Comprehensive core studies for the modern drummer

By Dave Hazlewood

Level One

Music by Dan Wright - Edited by Rob Woodcock

Knowle Farm Business Centre, Wadhurst Road,
Frant, Tunbridge Wells, Kent, TN3 9EJ
United Kingdom
www.one8e.co.uk • info@one8e.co.uk

ISBN 978-0-9567790-3-8

Backbone drums – Level 1
This volume: 2nd edition

Produced by one8e publishing
Published by one8e publishing

Printed and bound by CPI Group (UK) Ltd, Croydon, CRO 4YY

Edited by Rob Woodcock
Music by Dan Wright
Cover design by Andy McIntosh
Additional technical input from Mike Brazier
Cover photography by Mark Roe and David Brown
Internal photography by Mark Roe and Dan Wright

Backbone Drums

Introduction
Drums are the backbone of any band and the drummer has a vital part to play in making a successful band. This series of books is designed to be the backbone of a drummer's knowledge by looking into a huge number of concepts, techniques and styles. Not every element is covered in complete depth, but each gives an understanding and awareness of what is important for any drummer to know.

This is your 'Backbone' of knowledge
From here, you can choose to specialise or work in more depth on the things that you find most relevant and interesting. With many years of professional drumming experience, gigging, touring, recording and teaching, these books have been written and arranged in a practical order. The aim is to give the most realistic lesson structure to a student wanting to apply their drumming in the real world. This is not just about passing exams.

Backbone Drums: Level One.
Following on from the Foundation Level book, we will now look into more note values including eighth note triplets, sixteenth notes and off beats. We also start using the hi-hat pedal, look at tied notes and explore the concept of 'feel' in playing.

Contents

Backing track list

Backing tracks: Suitable for exercises from Chapter One

01 60bpm Modern blues
02 70bpm Classic blues
03 80bpm Triplet rock
04 85bpm Blues rock

Backing tracks: Suitable for exercises from Chapter Two onwards

05 60bpm Alt rock
06 65bpm Goth rock
07 70bpm Pop rap
08 75bpm Heavy rock
09 80bpm Modern disco
10 85bpm Groove pop
11 90bpm Early disco
12 95bpm Dance rock
13 100bpm Seventies disco
14 105bpm Nineties disco
15 110bpm Industrial dance
16 115bpm Disco pop
17 120bpm Synth pop

Chart tracks: To accompany the charts from Chapter Six

18 Chart 2 with drums
19 Chart 2 with click
20 Chart 4 with drums
21 Chart 4 with click
22 Chart 6 with drums
23 Chart 6 with click
24 Chart 7 with drums
25 Chart 7 with click

Click tracks: Suitable for exercises from any chapter

26 Click @ 60bpm
27 Click @ 65bpm
28 Click @ 70bpm
29 Click @ 75bpm
30 Click @ 80bpm
31 Click @ 85bpm
32 Click @ 90bpm
33 Click @ 95bpm
34 Click @ 100bpm
35 Click @ 105bpm
36 Click @ 110bpm
37 Click @ 115bpm
38 Click @ 120bpm

BPM: Beats Per Minute

Speed in music is called 'tempo' and is measured in 'beats per minute'. All backing tracks contain a click, which marks this time and occurs on every quarter note. Throughout this book, you'll see 'bpm', which has been written to either give you an idea of how fast you are playing or to give you goals to work towards.

Backing track guide

The first part of the CD contains backing tracks for you to play along with. There are several ways to use these, which will become more apparent the further you get through the book.

Groove playing

Initially looping one exercise along with a track will help to develop your timing and will be a great way to gauge your progress. When you feel you are ready to be more adventurous, return to this page to see how else you can use the backing tracks.

Four bar phrasing

Each section in all the backing tracks is written in groups of four bars, so you're able to loop four bar phrases all the way through a track and feel where the sections change without getting out of sync with the song.

Song structures

Backing tracks 1 and 2 are in a twelve-bar blues format. This is where a piece of music follows a particular chord progression over twelve bars, which gives it a very specific sound and is just like a twelve bar phrase.

Backing tracks 3 to 17 have the same structure.

A – Four bars – Intro/bridge (or extended chorus)
B – Four bars – Verse (part A)
B – Four bars – Verse (part B)
C – Four bars – Chorus

This arrangement is repeated four times.

Listen to the backing tracks to hear how the music changes from section to section, and then see how you can play each song more musically by playing a different groove for each section and fills that help move between them.

Chart writing

This is your chance to be really creative when writing drum parts, and will be a great exercise to prepare you for playing with a real band. If by the end of this book you are totally happy with reading music, you could try writing down your ideas in the form of a chart. Remember the arrangement (ABBC) is repeated four times and each time through doesn't have to be the same; feel free to experiment by maybe making the third time through completely different from the others.

Only attempt this if you are completely happy with everything in this book and you are working with a drum teacher, as this will be difficult to complete on your own with no guidance.

Reading and rudiment practice

Although the click tracks (26 to 38) are ideal for practicing reading exercises or rudiments, it's a good idea to play your own rudiments along with the musical backing tracks (with click) as well. Playing a paradiddle or double-stroke roll along with a rock track at 95bpm will be more interesting than playing to just a click at 95bpm, and will help you to develop a more musical feel.

Book guide

When giving note values their names, we have used a more modern system using fractions as names instead of giving them their more classical names. Although you don't need to know the classical names to work through this book, they are still used in certain situations so it's a good idea to learn them.

- Whole note – Semi-breve
- Half note – Minim
- Quarter note – Crotchet
- Eighth note – Quaver
- Sixteenth note – Semi Quaver

Note positions
The position of each drum and cymbal within the stave can vary in different publications as there has never been a universal standard. The positions used in this book have been the most common for most drummers and authors for some time now.

The stems of notes in written music can go up or down depending on where they sit on the stave. In drum music this is not always the case, but instead are written to be as easy to follow as possible.

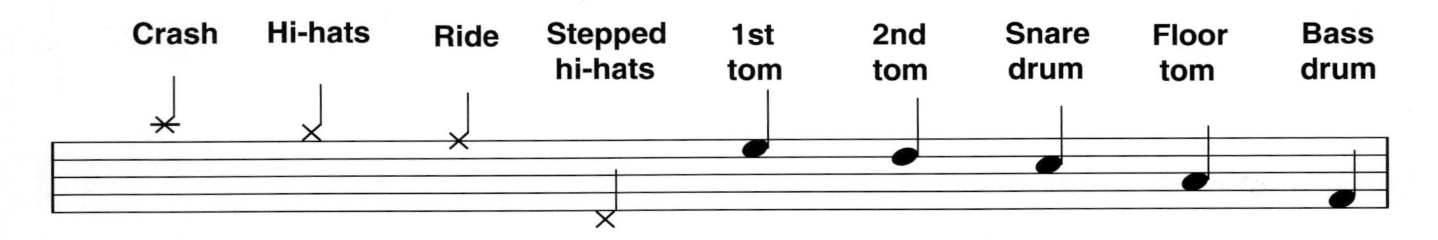

Left-handed drummers
Any exercise in this book that requires either a left or right hand to play a specific note has been written from a right-handed player's point of view. Left-handed players should reverse any instructions that state left and right.

Hi-hats or ride
Most of the grooves in this book are written with the cymbal part played on the hi-hats. A lot of these grooves will work just as well if played on the ride, so feel free to experiment.

Signing off and moving on
At the bottom of most pages within this book and the rest of the series, you will see a section titled 'Signing off and moving on'. These have targets that you should aim to achieve before moving on. They are broken down into Bronze, Silver and Gold; with Bronze being the minimum requirement, Silver being acceptable and Gold being a good standard at which to progress. Faster is not always better though, so make sure you sign off each target. Although it's preferable to sign off at gold standard before moving on, it's not essential, and if you are struggling with any section, you should just make a note of what level you have achieved and move on. You can always go back to review weaker sections at a later date.

Teachers subscribing to the online lesson manager application will be able to record Gold, Silver and Bronze awards for each student using the progress records. These will show at a glance which areas need more attention and practice.

Three's a crowd

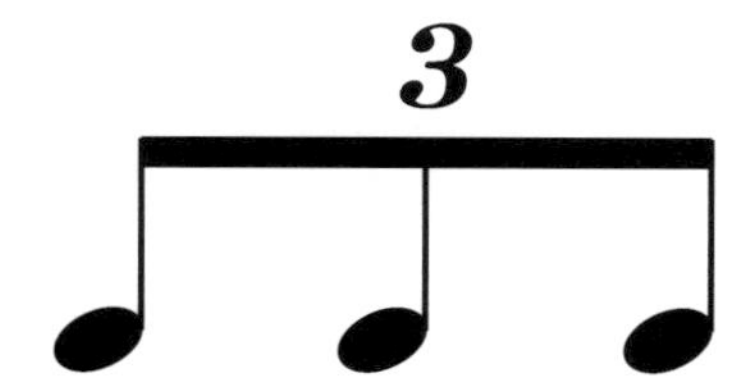

Eighth note triplets
(Quaver triplets)

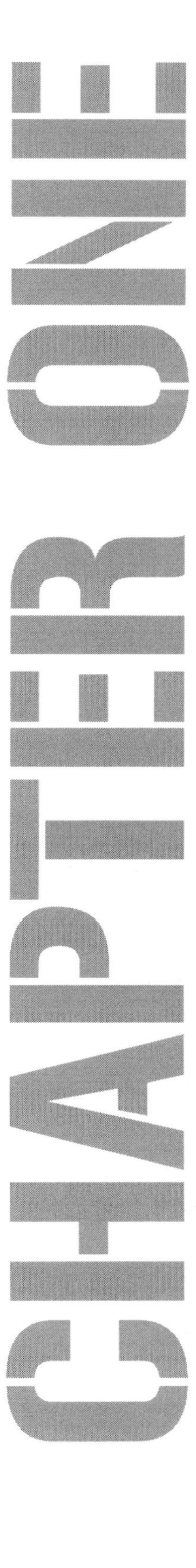

First up, we are going to look at some grooves and fills that are a bit different to anything we looked at in the Foundation book. These are 'triplet' notes, which are notes in groups of three that have a very different feel.

Checklist

By the end of this chapter, you should be able to achieve the following:

- Play eighth note triplet grooves
- Play eighth note triplet fills
- Play along with triplet feel backing tracks
- Read music containing quarter notes and eighth note triplets
- Play fills mixing quarter notes and eighth note triplets
- Create your own fills mixing quarter notes and eighth note triplets

Use this page as an end-of-chapter test. When you have completed Chapter One, come back to this page and see if you can complete the list above.

Eighth note triplet groove

The eighth notes we looked at in the previous book had a very straight and even feel to them, and are written in groups of two or four. These notes work well in a lot of musical situations, but not all. A lot of music has a 'swing' or 'shuffle' feel to it and requires different notes to work. This is where triplet notes come in which are grouped into threes and give music a 'swing'.

Every note value has an equivalent 'triplet' brother, (quarter note triplets, half note triplets, and so on), which means for every two 'non-triplet' notes, there'll be three notes in its triplet version. There's a new way to count eighth-note triplets; when counted out loud this will sound like: '1anah, 2anah, 3anah, 4anah'.

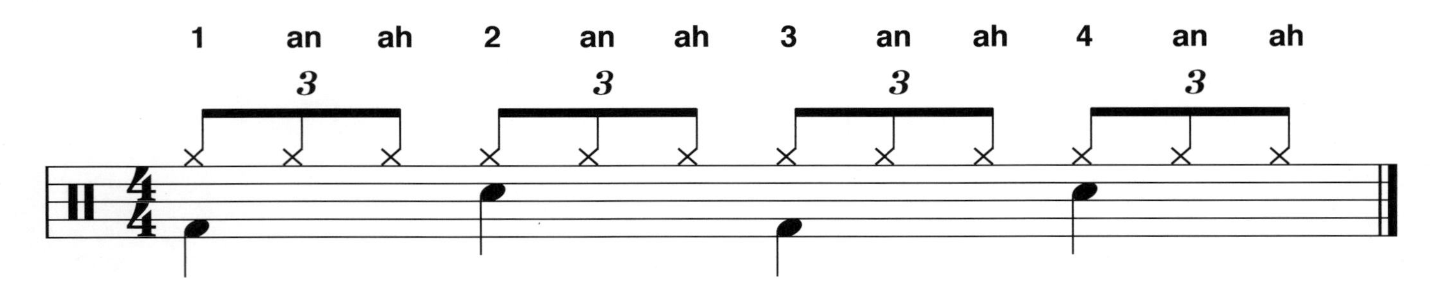

Practice this groove with backing tracks and really focus on making sure that your notes are nice and even. A row of eighth note triplets should be as even as a row of eighth notes. Avoid any awkward rhythms or pauses when you are playing (try saying 'pineapple, pineapple, pineapple, pineapple with no pauses).

Eighth note triplet fill

Eighth note triplets also work well in fills, but the sticking may initially feel slightly strange as your lead hand isn't always in time with the pulse. Loop the bar below with your bass drum playing every quarter note to develop even eighth note triplets, and get used to your weaker hand playing in time with the pulse.

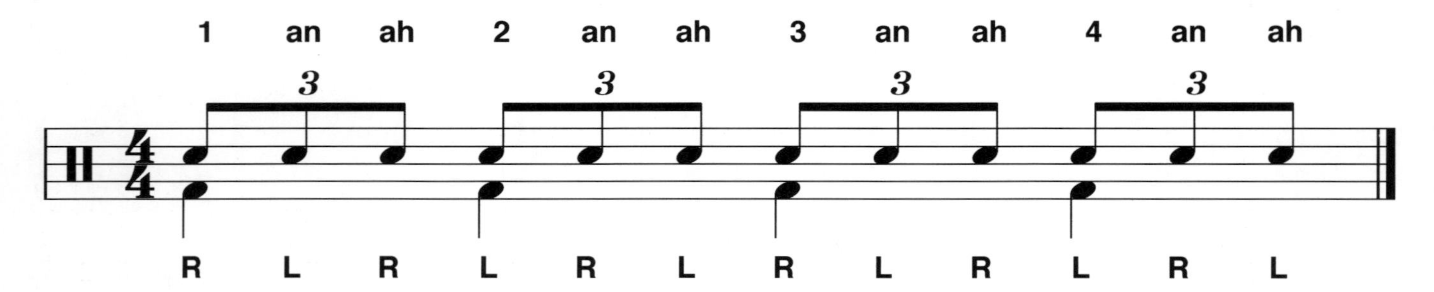

Signing off and moving on

Play the eighth note triplet groove along with suitable backing tracks
Targets are in BPM

60	65	70	75	80	85	90	95	100	105	110	115	120
Bronze		Silver			Gold							

Now play the eighth note triplets around the drums as a fill. Note that the last group of three is played back on the first tom to avoid crossing your arms.

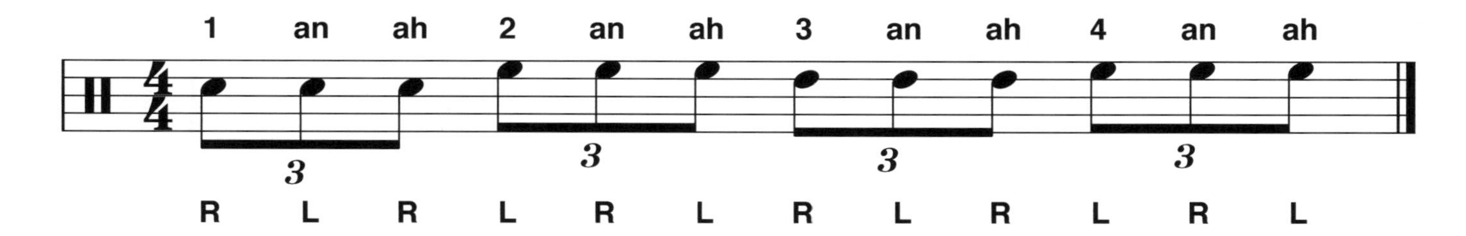

Four bar phrase

When you are happy playing the groove and fill at a constant speed, play them both in four bar phrases. The groove is written to be played on the hi-hats, but will also sound nice on the ride, so play it both ways.

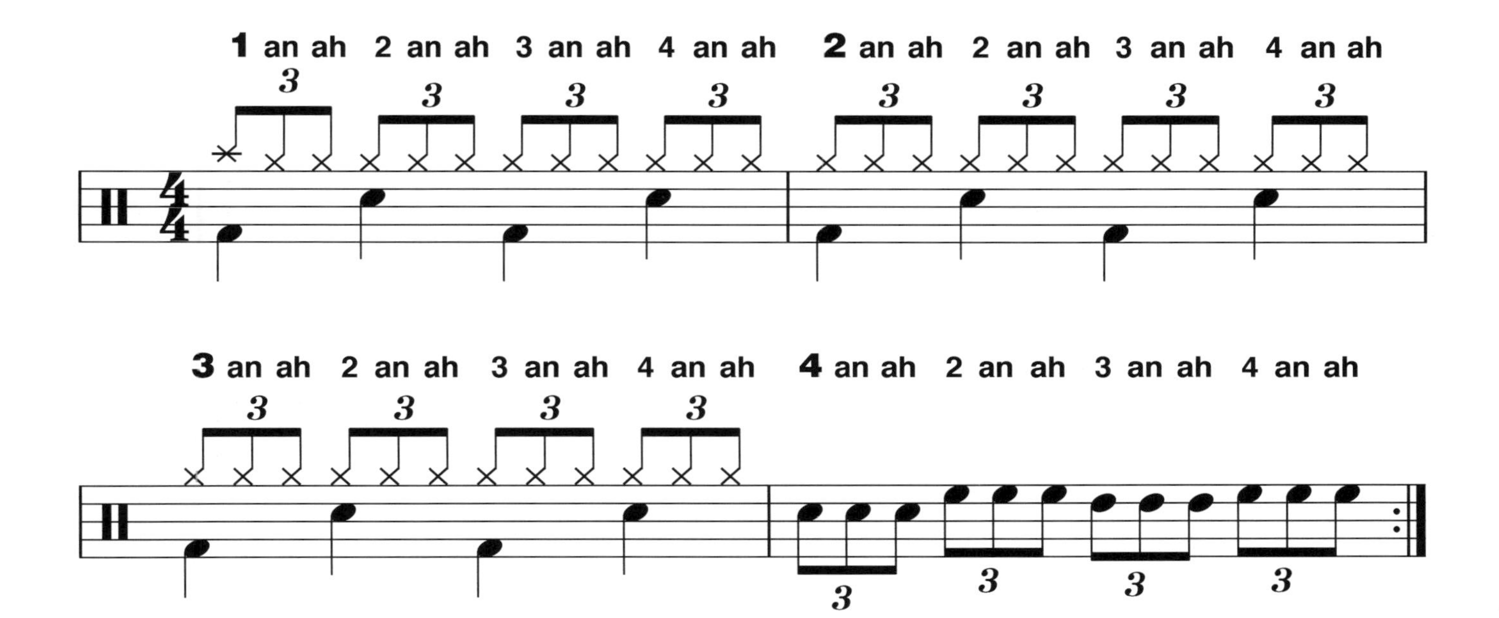

Signing off and moving on

Play the above four bar phrase along with suitable backing tracks
Targets are in BPM

60	65	70	75	80	85	90	95	100	105	110	115	120
Bronze		Silver			Gold							

Reading exercises for the snare drum

You can play eighth note triplets with any other notes, but this can create some timing issues, so for now we are only going to mix them with quarter notes. Play the following exercises one at a time and then play the whole page. Make sure that you have a strong count and keep the numbers even with the in-between counts well spaced.

Sticking: Below each exercise is a suggested sticking pattern, which will help make your rhythms flow and will hopefully make the page easier to play as a whole piece.

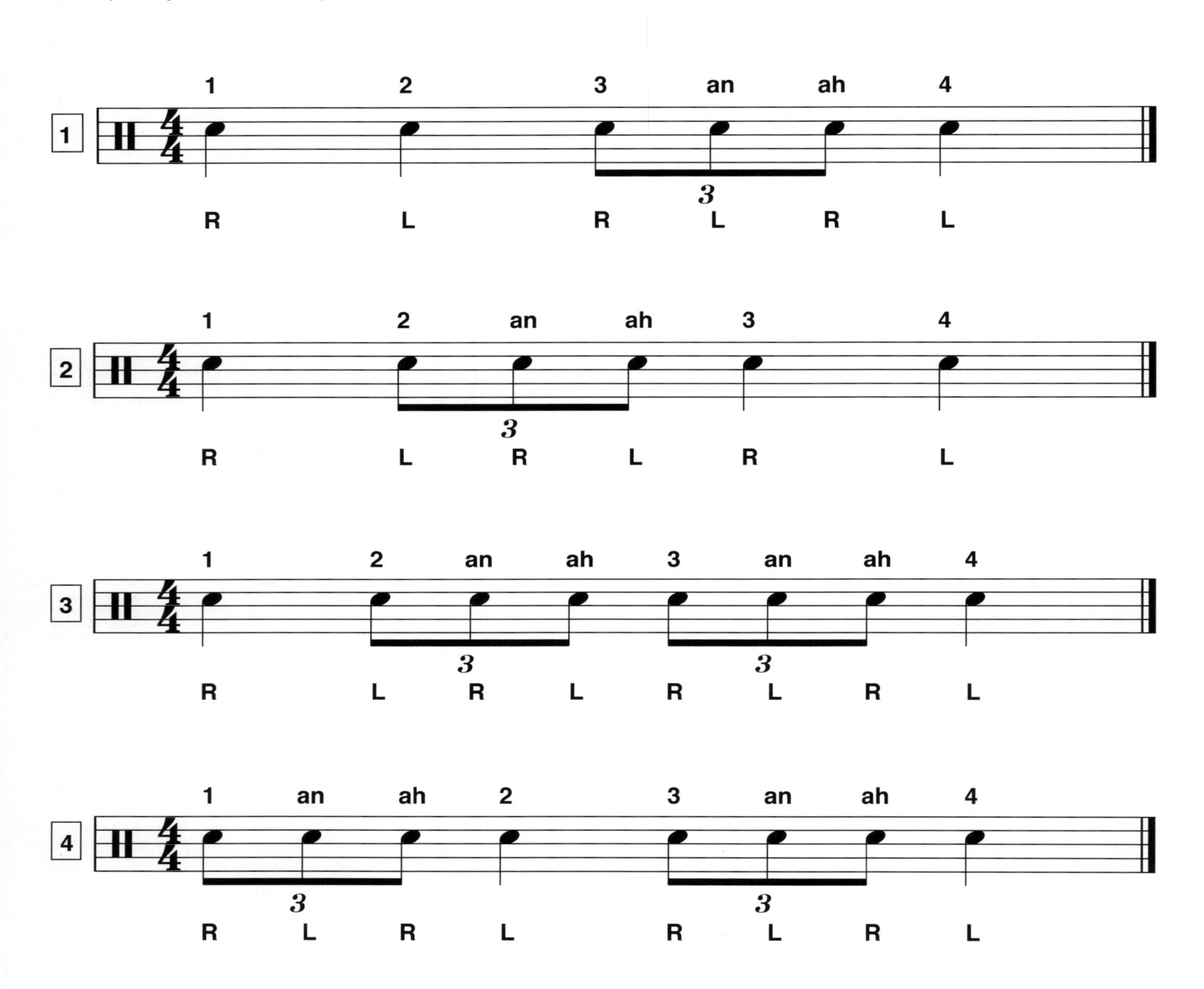

Signing off and moving on

Play the entire page as one exercise, with a click track
Targets are in BPM

60	65	70	75	80	85	90	95	100	105	110	115	120
Bronze					Silver					Gold		

Reading exercises as fills

Taking the rhythms from the previous page, we can start to play them around the drums in fills. Play the following fills on their own to start with, and then play in four bar phrases, with the eighth note triplet groove. As you gain confidence and increase the tempo, you'll find that the quarter note groove from Chapter One of the previous book works really well instead of an eighth note triplet groove.

Sticking: Pay attention to which hand is leading on which drum.

Signing off and moving on

Play each fill with the eighth note triplet groove in four bar phrases along with suitable backing tracks
Targets are in BPM

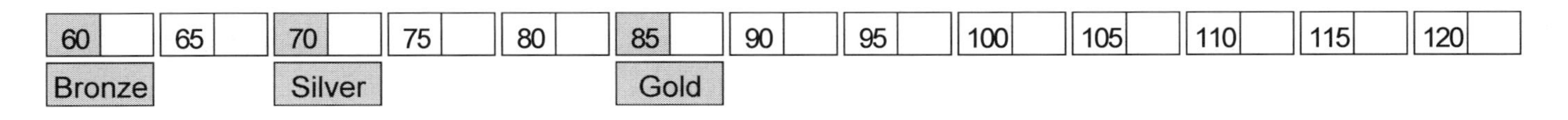

Create your own fills

Use these blank staves to make your own rhythms, which you can then play around the drums as fills.

Sticking: Write the sticking underneath each of your ideas to help make them flow.

Use the following rhythms:

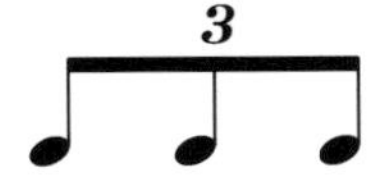

1
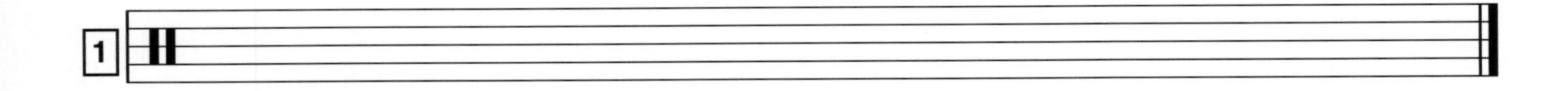

2
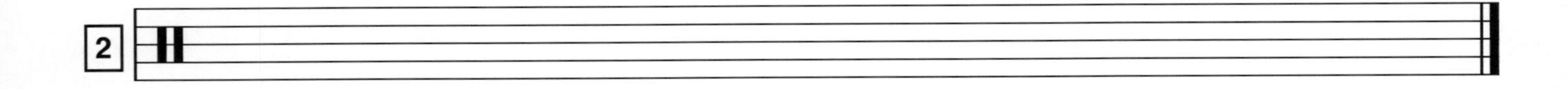

3
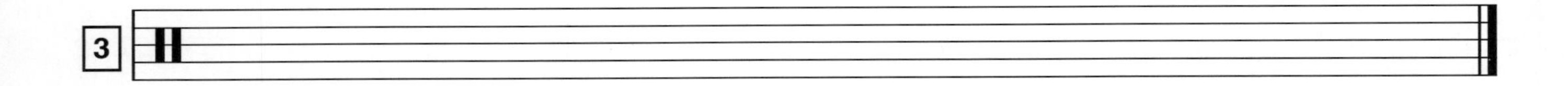

4
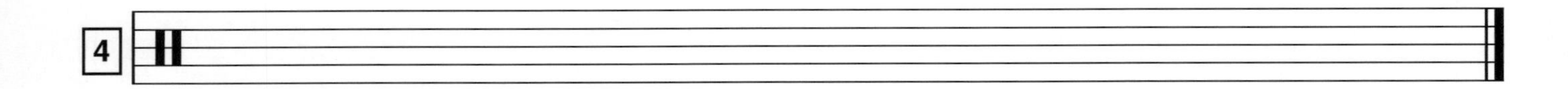

Signing off and moving on

Play each fill with the eighth note triplet groove in four-bar phrases along with suitable backing tracks
Targets are in BPM

60	65	70	75	80	85	90	95	100	105	110	115	120
Bronze		Silver			Gold							

Triplet rudiments

In the previous book, we looked at rudiments using eighth notes, so here are some rudiments using eighth note triplets. Although they are not all official rudiments, they are useful to learn. Practice slowly with a click, and focus on technique and achieving a good sound rather than just trying to play faster.

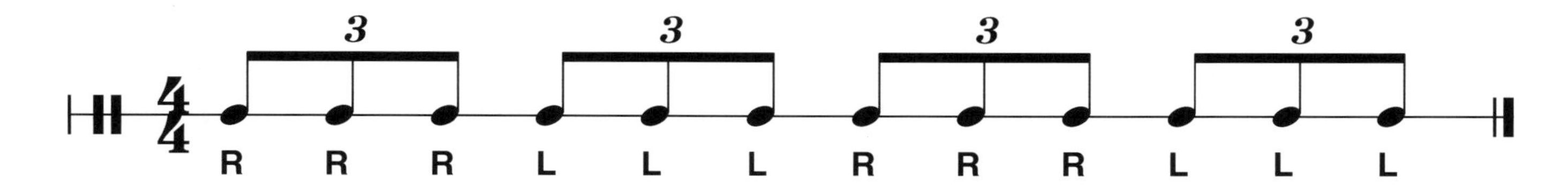

Other useful stickings

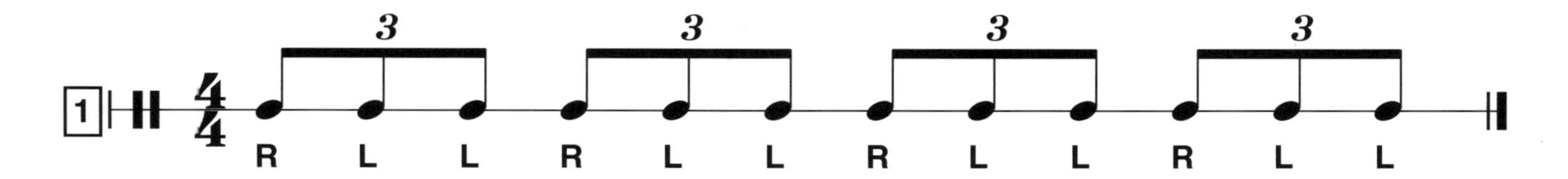

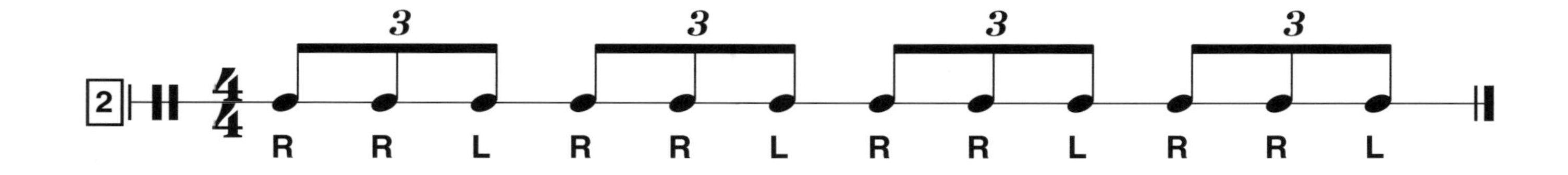

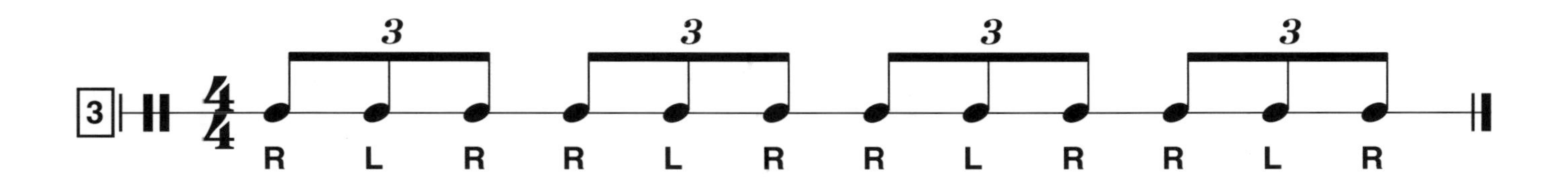

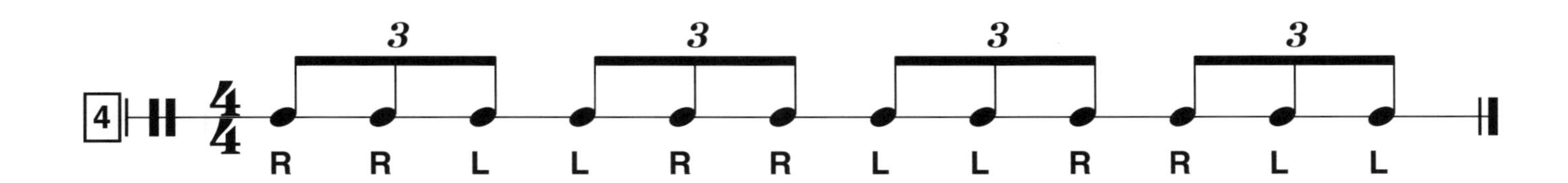

Signing off and moving on

Play each exercise with a click track
Targets are in BPM

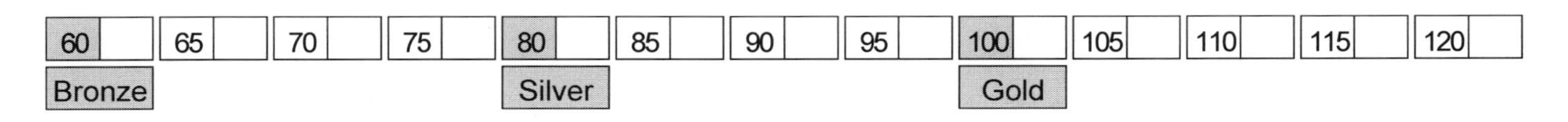

Triplet rudiments in fills

Here are some ideas of how these rudiments can be played in fills. Play each of them in four-bar phrases.

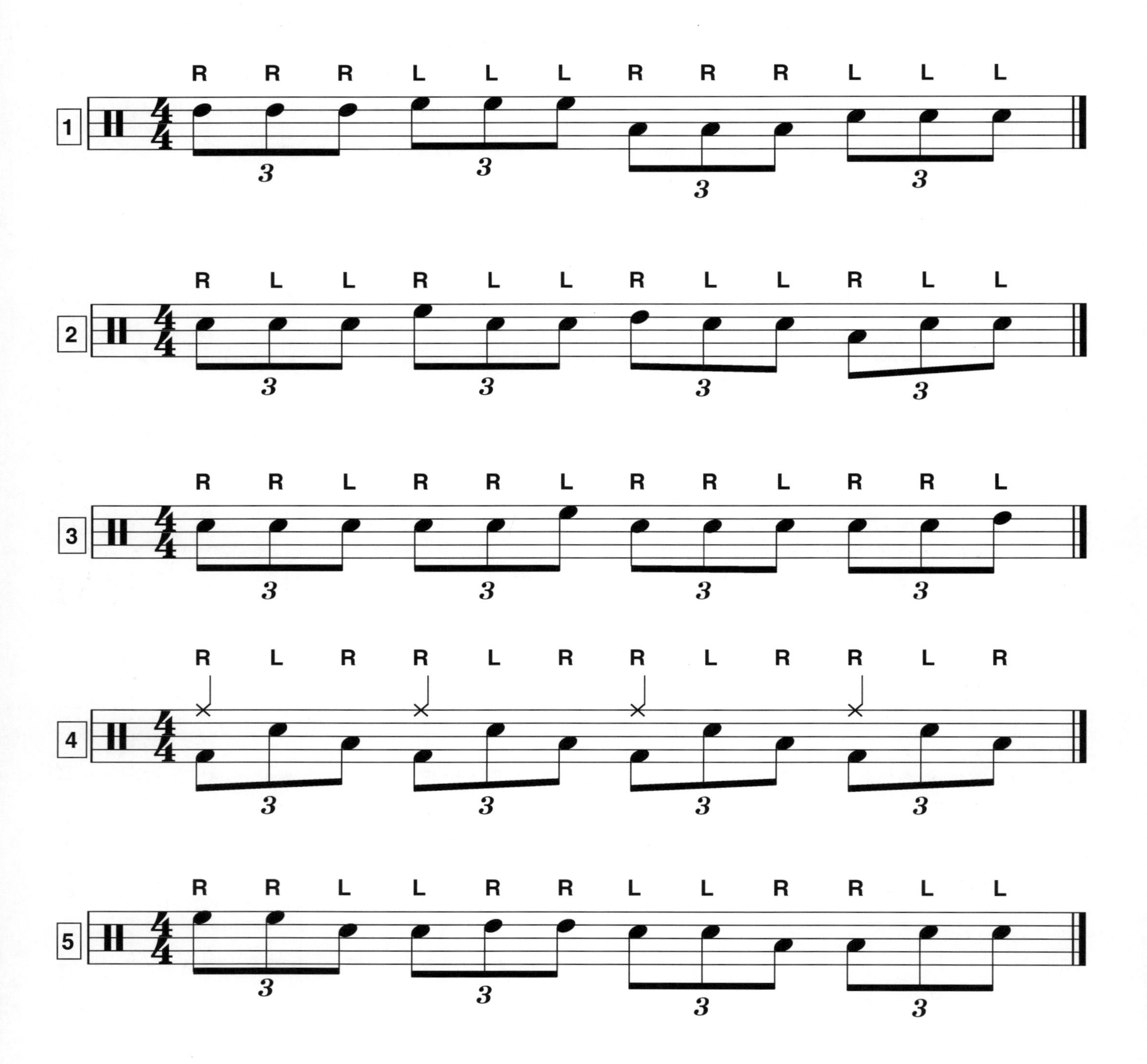

Signing off and moving on

Play each fill with the eighth note triplet groove in four-bar phrases along with suitable backing tracks
Targets are in BPM

60	65	70	75	80	85	90	95	100	105	110	115	120
Bronze		Silver			Gold							

Make room for some more

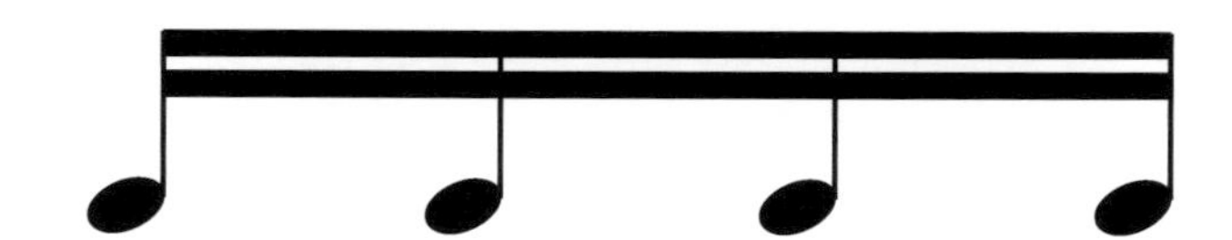

A sixteenth note (Semi-quaver)

Four sixteenth notes joined (Four semi-quavers)

In Chapter Two, we are going to look at some new notes called sixteenth notes. Just as other notes we have looked at, these get their names from their relationship to a whole note. Therefore, there are sixteen sixteenth notes to a whole note. A single sixteenth note looks different to an eighth note because it has two tails instead of just one.

Checklist

By the end of this chapter, you should be able to achieve the following:

- Play sixteenth note grooves
- Play sixteenth note fills
- Read music containing quarter notes, eighth notes and sixteenth notes
- Play fills mixing quarter notes, eighth notes and sixteenth notes
- Create your own fills mixing quarter notes, eighth notes and sixteenth notes
- Play some different bass drum patterns with sixteenth note hi-hats
- Play rudiments over sixteenth notes

Use this page as an end-of-chapter test. When you've finished Chapter Two, come back to this page and see if you can complete the list above.

Sixteenth note groove

This next groove uses the first rudiment we looked at in the previous book, the single stroke roll. You are now going to play so many notes that to play at a reasonable speed; you will need to use both hands on the hi-hats. This also means your lead hand will be playing the snare drum and the hi-hat.

Notice the new counting system above the hi-hats used to incorporate all of these notes.

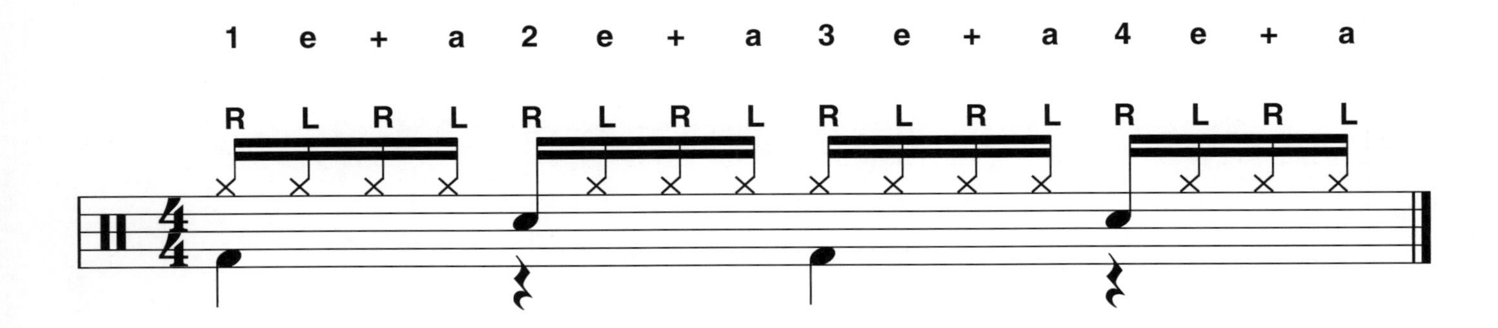

Sixteenth note fill

As well as using sixteenth notes in grooves, we can play them in fills. Here's a basic fill using sixteenth notes.

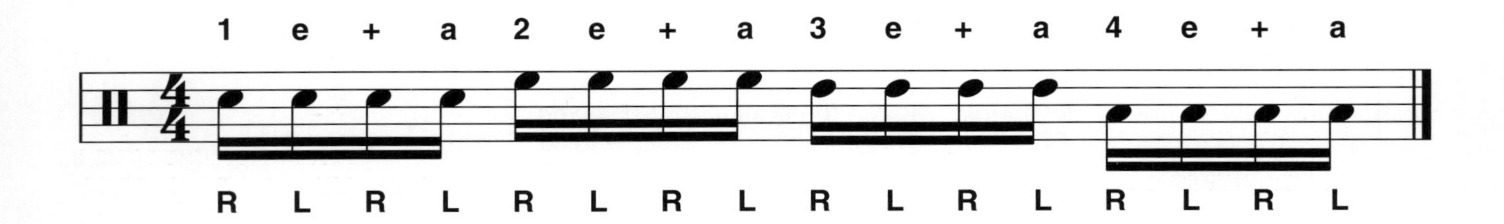

Signing off and moving on

Play the sixteenth note groove along with suitable backing tracks
Targets are in BPM

60	65	70	75	80	85	90	95	100	105	110	115	120
Bronze			Silver			Gold						

Sixteenth note four bar phrase

Here is the groove and fill together in a four bar phrase. When you play the crash at the start of each four bar phrase make sure your following hand is already on the way back to the hi-hats.

One-handed sixteenth note groove

It's worth noting at this point that it's possible to play the sixteenth note groove with just your lead hand, but it will obviously be much slower. Play the following four bar phrase, with the groove on the ride with just your lead hand, and then play the fill with both hands.

Signing off and moving on

Play the top four bar phrase along with suitable backing tracks
Targets are in BPM

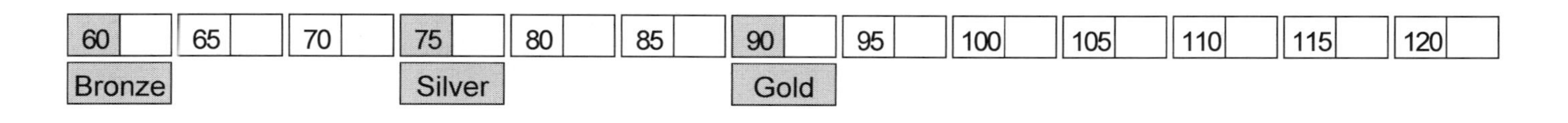

Reading exercises for the snare drum

Here are some exercises which mix quarter, eighth and sixteenth notes. Playing these exercises with a click track at different tempos is a great way to help develop your timing. Play the following exercises one at a time and then play the whole page as one piece.

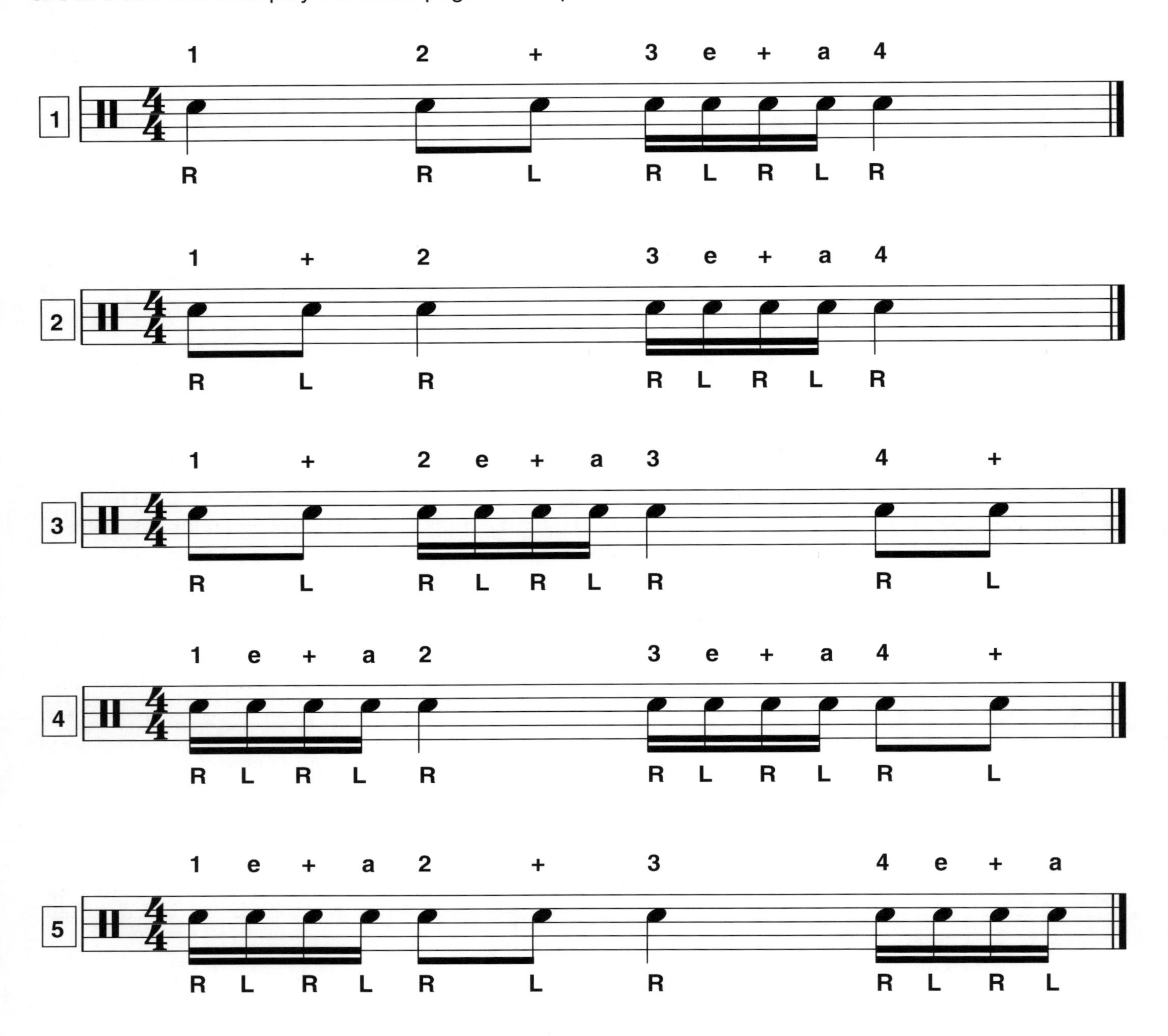

Signing off and moving on

Play the entire page as one exercise with a click track

Targets are in BPM

60	65	70	75	80	85	90	95	100	105	110	115	120
Bronze						Silver						Gold

Reading exercises as fills

Now you are comfortable with the timing of playing quarter, eighth and sixteenth notes together, we can start to play the same rhythms around the drums in our fills. Play these fills with quarter, eighth and sixteenth note grooves

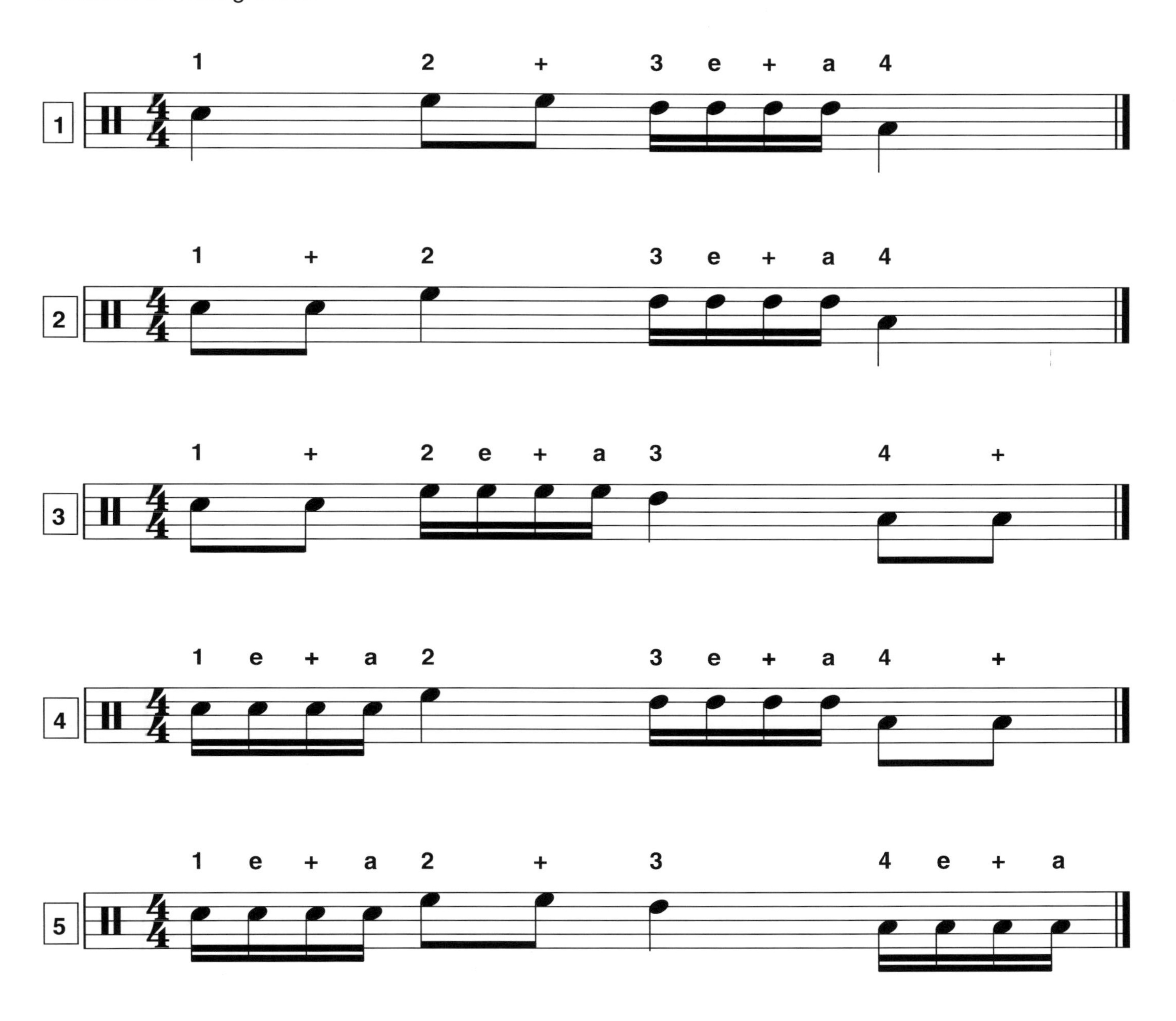

Signing off and moving on

Play each fill above with quarter or eighth note grooves in four bar phrases, with suitable backing tracks
Targets are in BPM

60	65	70	75	80	85	90	95	100	105	110	115	120
Bronze						Silver						Gold

Create your own fills

Use the blank staves below to make your own rhythms, which you can then play around the drums as fills.

Use the following rhythms:  

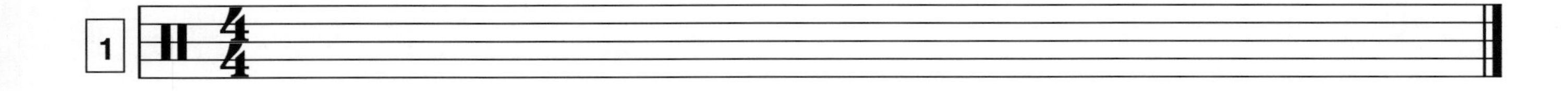

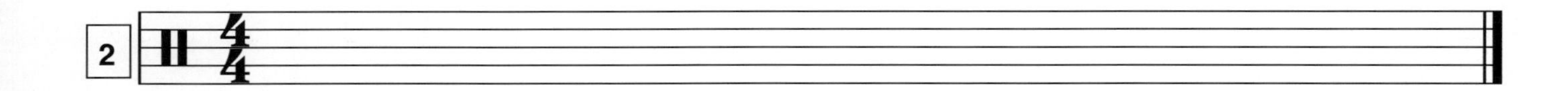

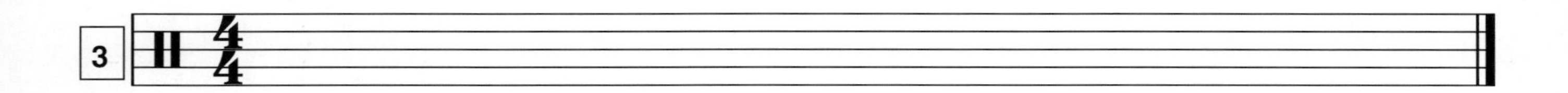

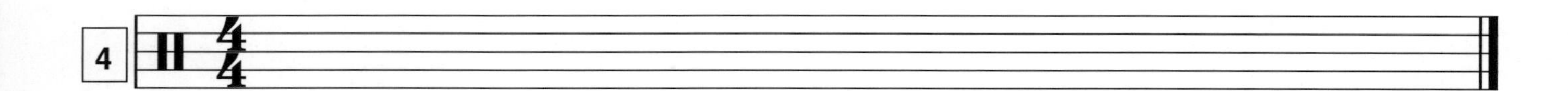

Signing off and moving on

Play each of the fills above in four bar phrases along with suitable backing tracks
Targets are in BPM

60	65	70	75	80	85	90	95	100	105	110	115	120
Bronze						Silver						Gold

Sixteenth note grooves with varied bass drum patterns

Here are some sixteenth note grooves now with more interesting and challenging bass drum patterns.

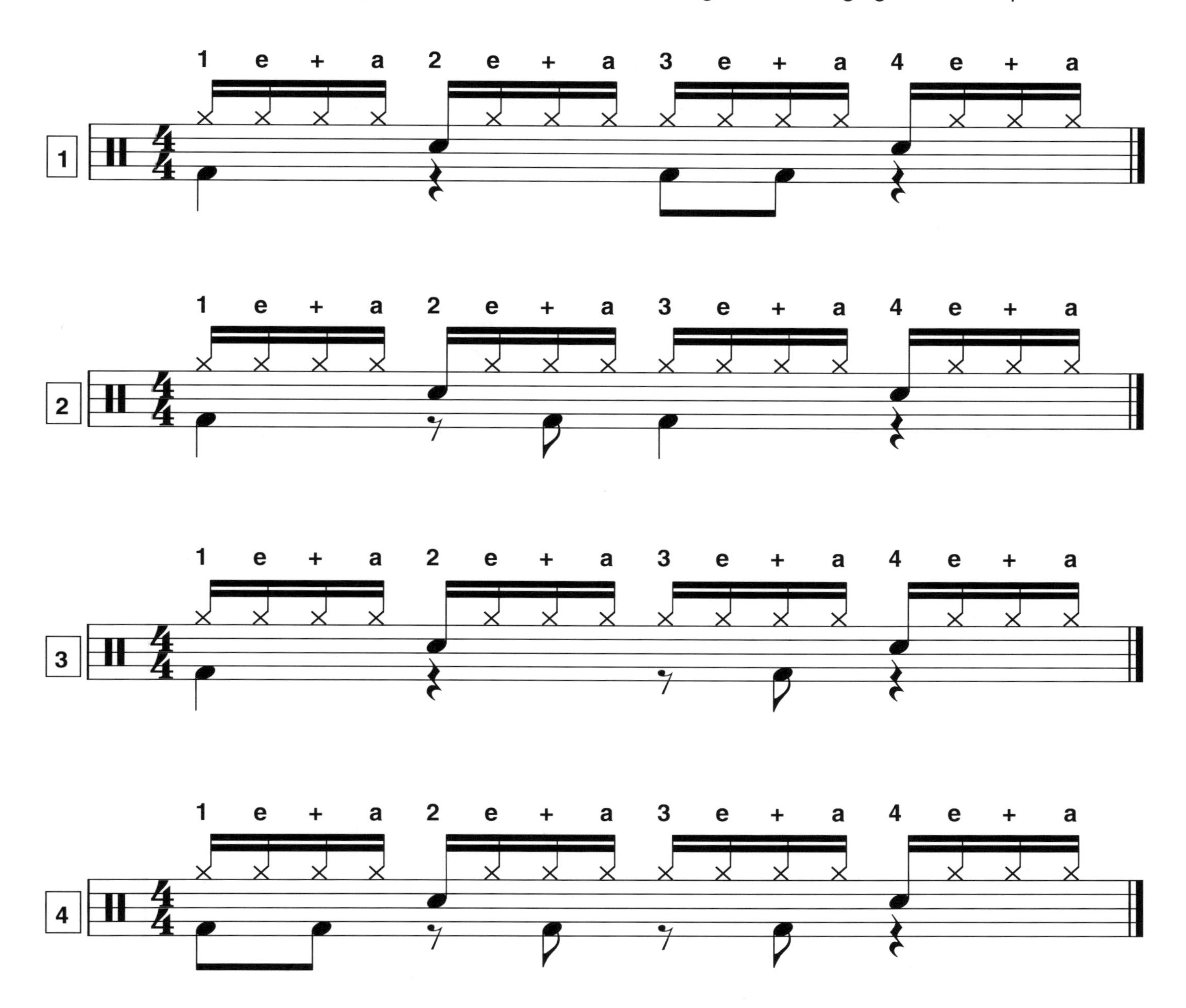

Signing off and moving on

Play each of the grooves above along with suitable backing tracks
Targets are in BPM

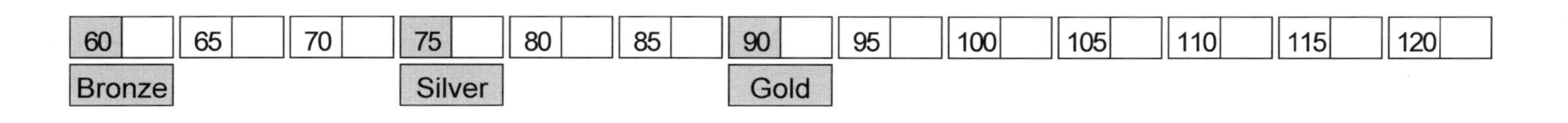

Rudiments over sixteenth notes

In the previous book we looked at three rudiments, which we played as eighth notes. Let's now look at those and some new rudiments played over sixteenth notes. Still focusing on good technique, great sound and even notes, we can now see if we can increase how fast we play these rudiments.

Single stroke roll

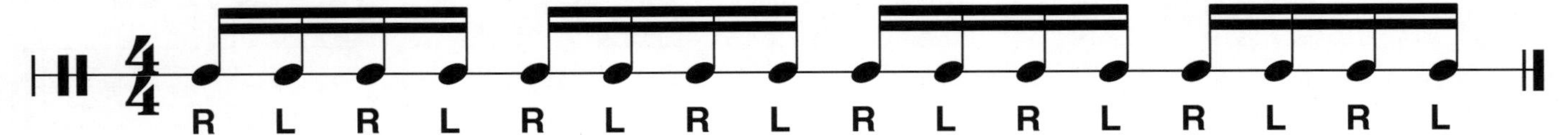

Double stroke roll

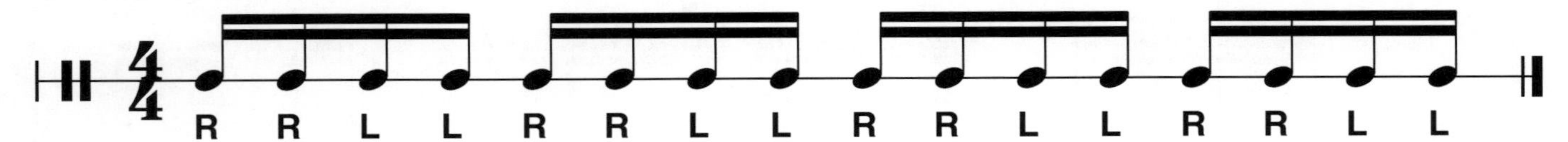

Paradiddle

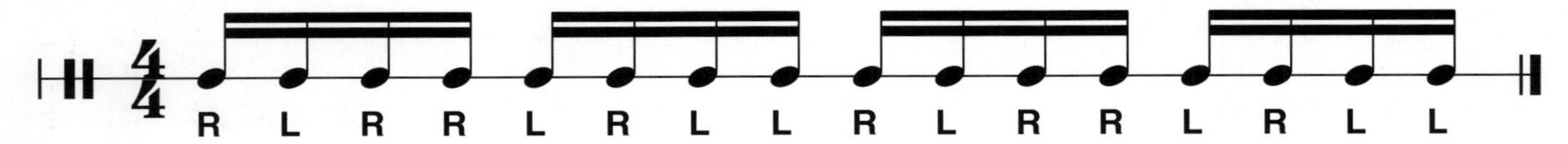

Inverted paradiddle

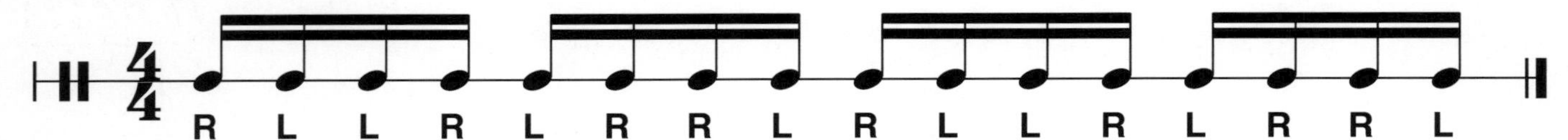

Reversed paradiddle

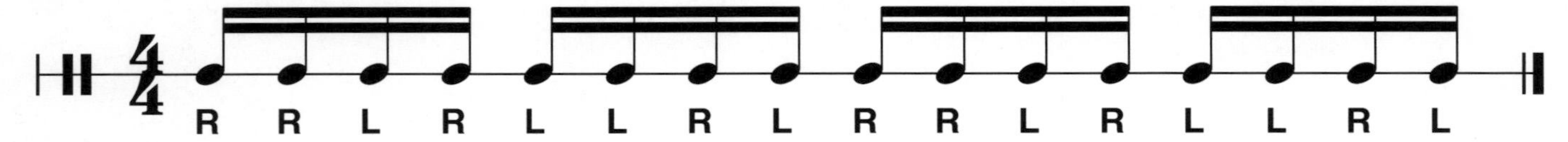

Signing off and moving on

Play each exercise with a click track

Targets are in BPM

60	65	70	75	80	85	90	95	100	105	110	115	120
Bronze			Silver			Gold						

Off the beaten track

Eighth note rest
(Quaver rest)

Eighth note
(Quaver)

Nearly everything we have looked at so far has involved playing on the pulse to develop a good sense of timing. In this chapter, we'll start to look at grooves and fills that fall mainly off of the pulse, also known as playing off-beats.

Checklist

By the end of this chapter, you should be able to achieve the following:

- Play off-beat eighth note grooves
- Play off-beat eighth note fills
- Read rhythms that include off-beats
- Create your own fills using off-beats
- Play more interesting bass drum patterns within grooves
- Create your own grooves using off-beats

Use this page as an end-of-chapter test. When you have completed Chapter Three, come back to this page and see if you can complete the list above.

Off-beat eighth note groove

Here's our first groove that relies heavily on playing off-beats. You'll notice that the snare and bass drums are played in exactly the same places as every other groove we've played, but the hi-hats are only played on the off-beat. This places a hi-hat in between every bass and snare.

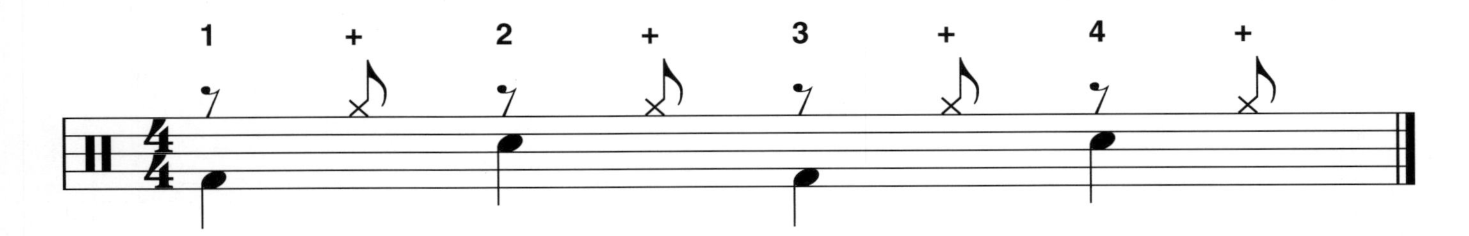

Off-beat eighth note fill

Here's a fill made up of off-beats. Play it with a click track and count out loud, focusing on placing each hit exactly between each count (on the 'and' of each count) before you attempt to play it with the groove.

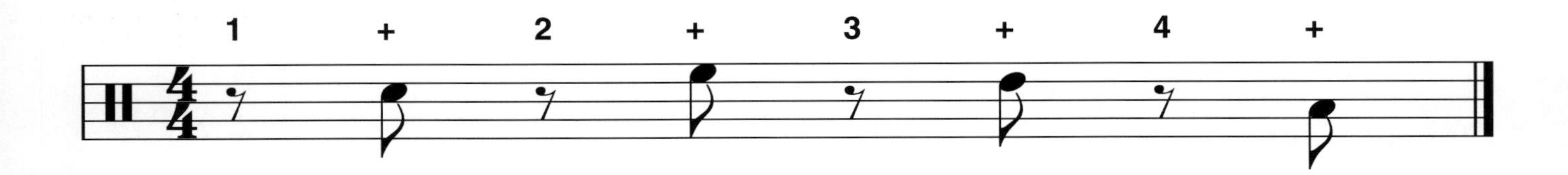

Signing off and moving on

Play the off-beat eighth note groove along with suitable backing tracks
Targets are in BPM

60	65	70	75	80	85	90	95	100	105	110	115	120
Bronze					Silver					Gold		

Off-beat eighth note four bar phrase

Now play the groove and fill in four bar phrases. Watch out for the crash on beat 1, which will be the only cymbal played on the beat.

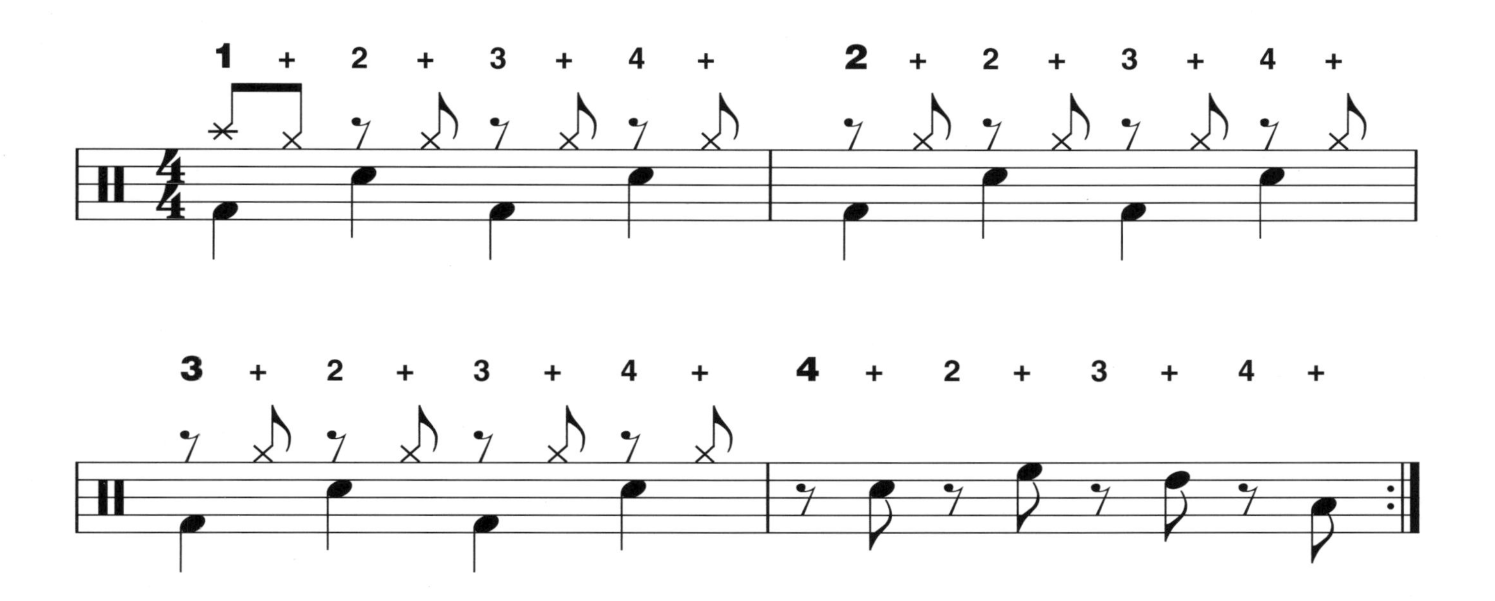

Signing off and moving on

Play the four bar phrase along with suitable backing tracks
Targets are in BPM

60	65	70	75	80	85	90	95	100	105	110	115	120
Bronze					Silver					Gold		

Reading Exercises For The Snare Drum

By mixing off-beats with other notes we have been using, we can create some really interesting rhythms. Play the following exercises individually with a click track and then play the whole page as one exercise.

Sticking: Good practice is to play on-beats with your lead hand and off-beats with your following hand.

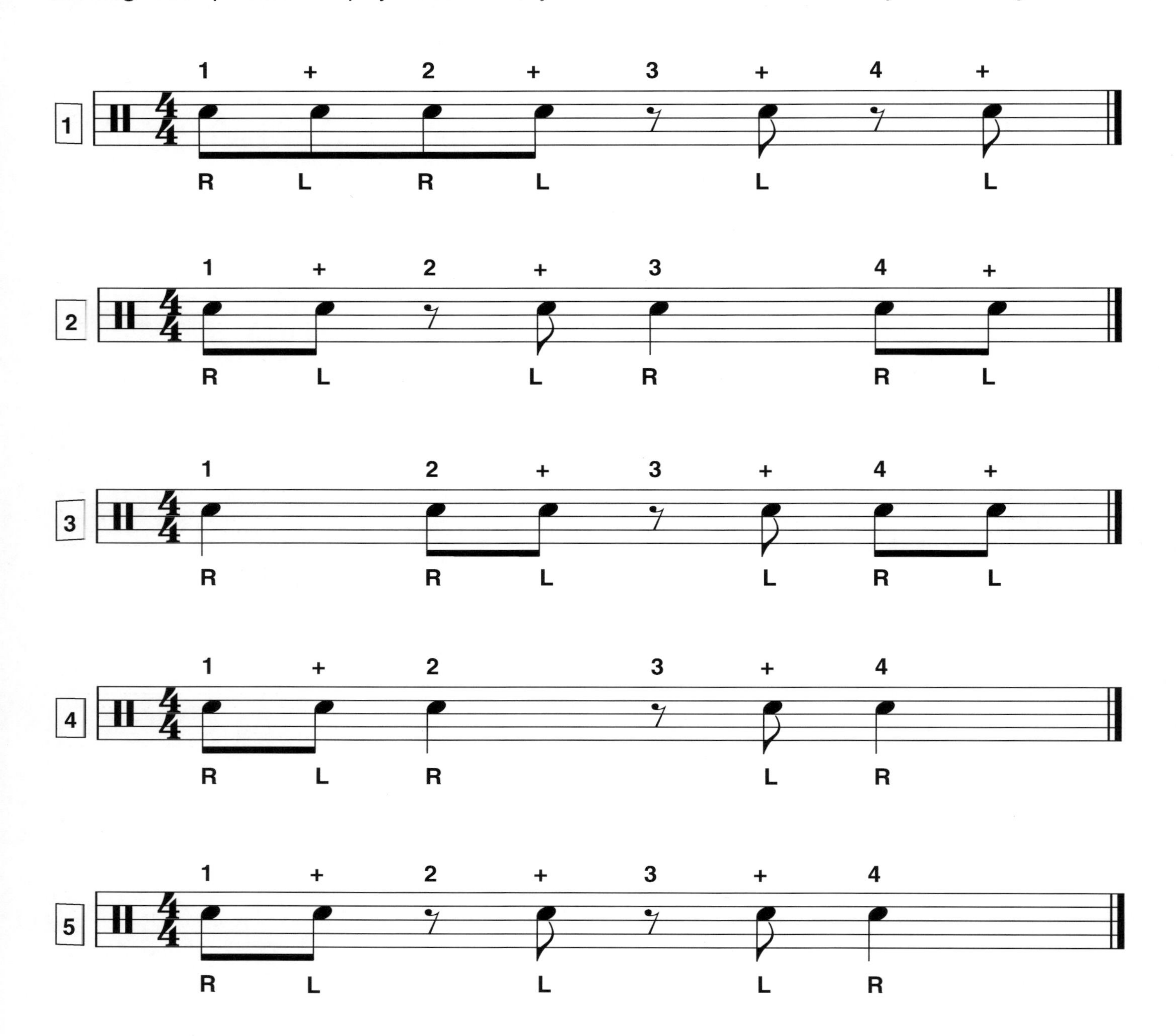

Signing off and moving on

Play the entire page as one exercise with a click track
Targets are in BPM

60	65	70	75	80	85	90	95	100	105	110	115	120
Bronze						Silver						Gold

Reading exercises as fills

Play the same rhythms from the previous page around the drums as fills to add space and musicality to your playing.

Play these fills with standard quarter and eighth note grooves in four bar phrases.

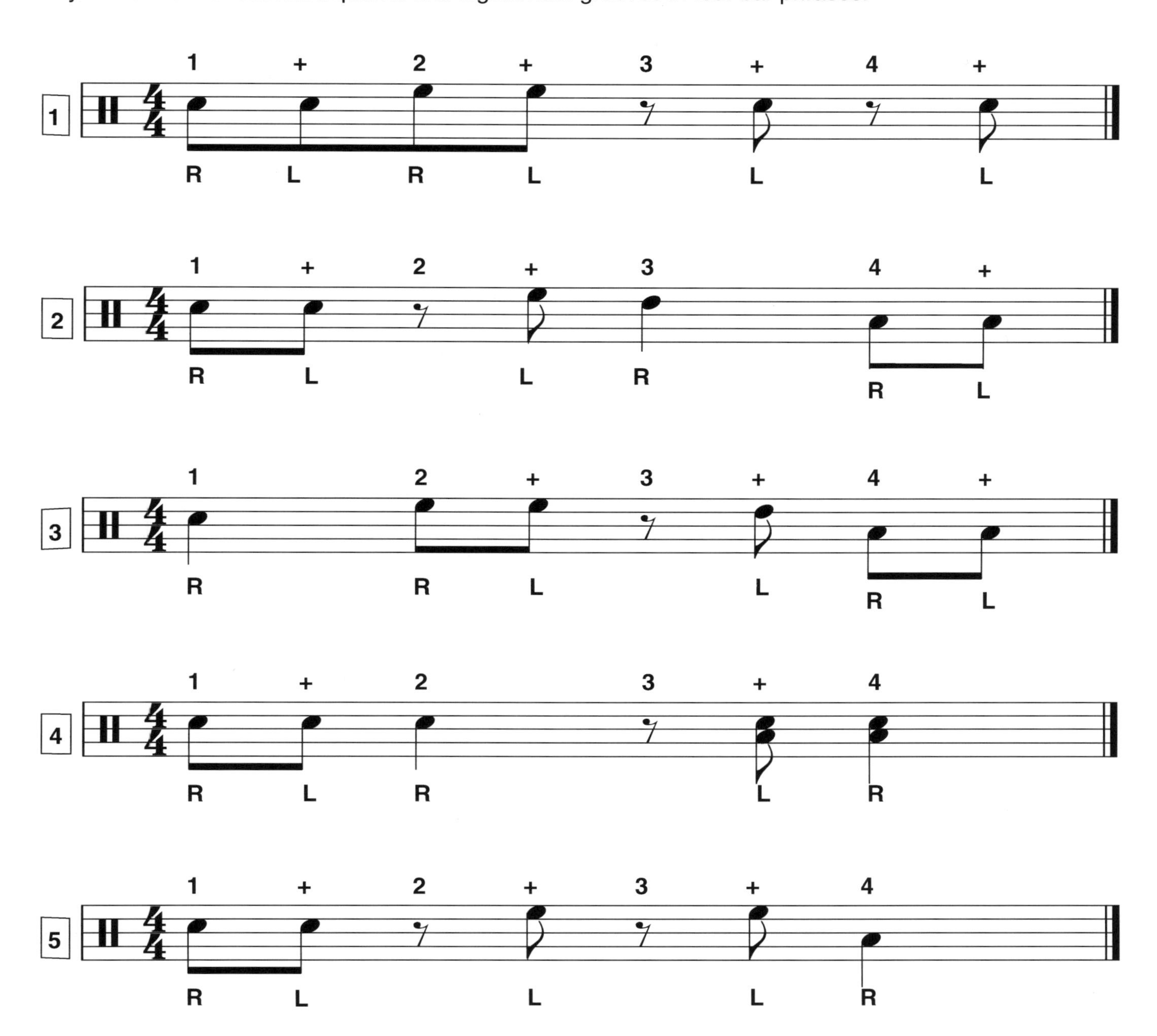

Signing off and moving on

Play each fill above with quarter or eighth note grooves in four bar phrases with suitable backing tracks
Targets are in BPM

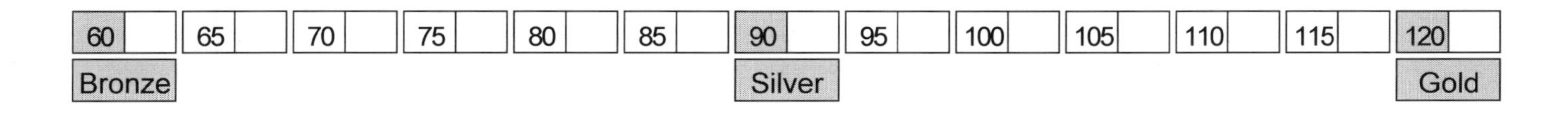

Create your own fills

Use the blank staves below to make your own rhythms, which you can then play around the drums as fills.

Use the following rhythms:

1

2

3

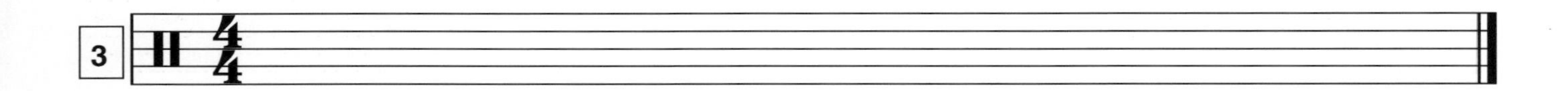

4

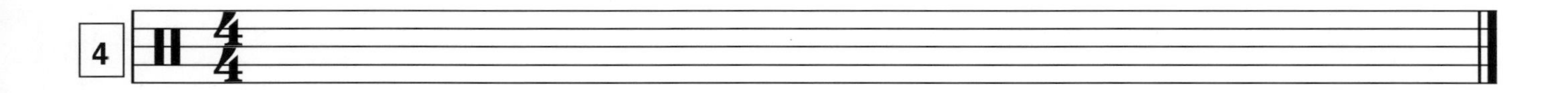

Signing off and moving on

Play each of the fills above in four bar phrases along with suitable backing tracks

Targets are in BPM

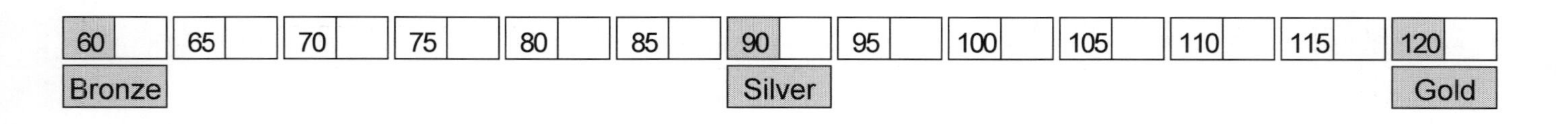

Off-beat grooves

Here are some more interesting and challenging off-beat grooves. Loop each one with backing tracks and then play in four bar phrases with simple fills.

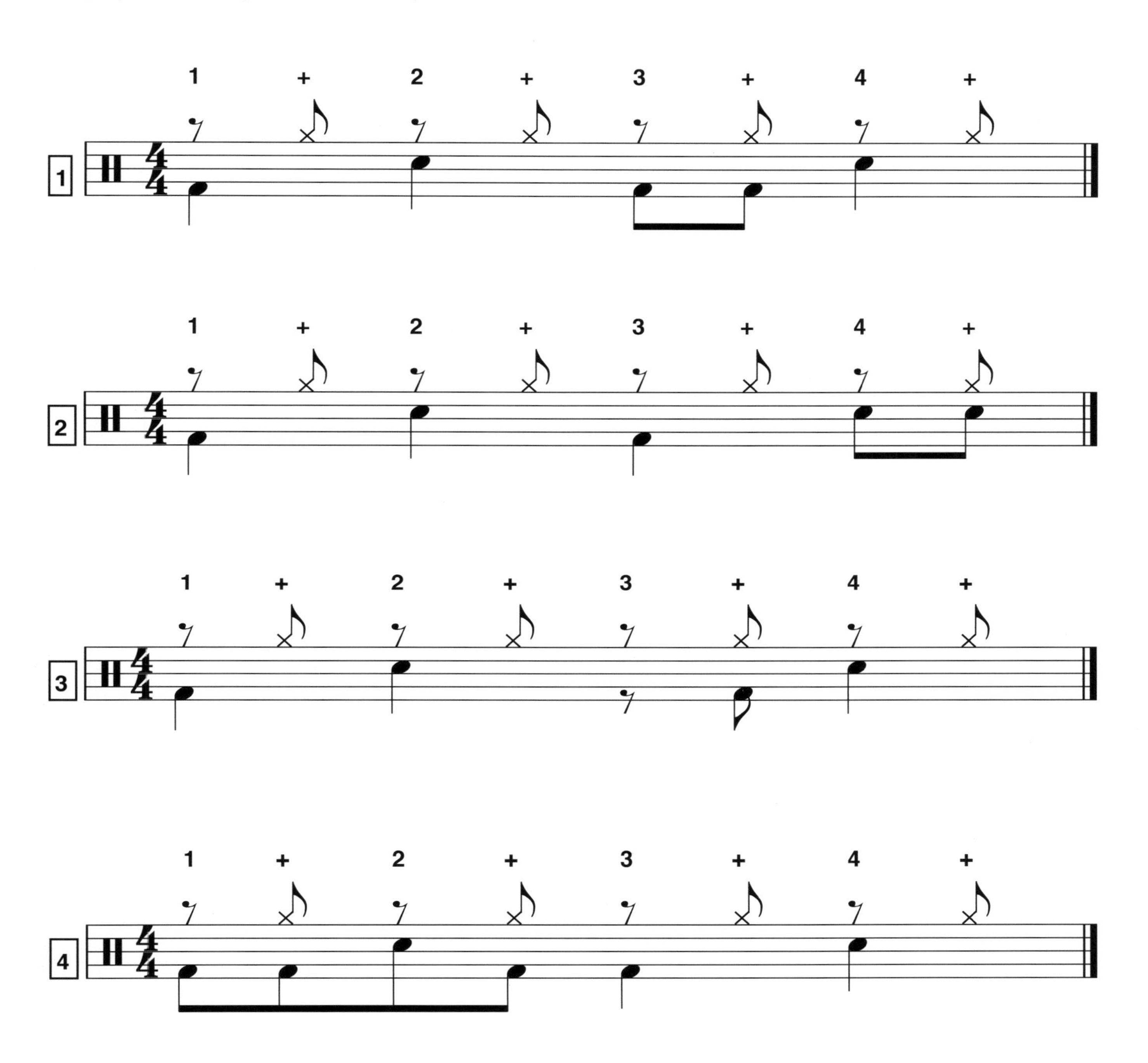

Signing off and moving on

Play each of the grooves above along with suitable backing tracks
Targets are in BPM

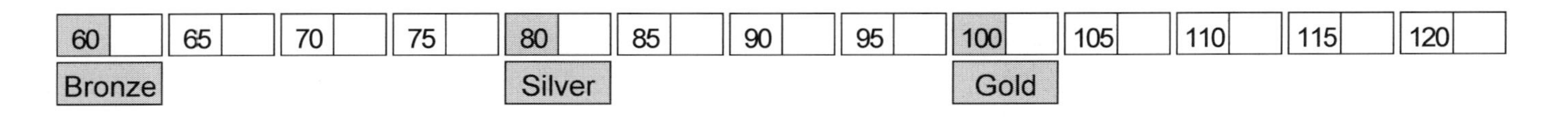

Two bar phrases

Up until now, we've always looped a single groove when playing along with backing tracks, either with or without fills. A common variation though, is to join two similar grooves together and loop them in what we call a two bar phrase. This can create a nice feel and make our grooves even more musical.

Loop each of the following two bar phrases with backing tracks. There's no need to add fills at this stage.

Signing off and moving on

Play each of the two bar phrases above along with suitable backing tracks
Targets are in BPM

60	65	70	75	80	85	90	95	100	105	110	115	120
Bronze				Silver				Gold				

The missing link

In Chapter Four, we move from three to four-way co-ordination, as we start to use the hi-hat pedal.

Checklist

By the end of this chapter, you should be able to achieve the following:

- Understand the various ways in which the hi-hat pedal can be employed
- Play grooves with hi-hat lifts in various parts of the bar
- Utilise the hi-hat pedal to create different textures

Use this page as an end-of-chapter test. When you've completed Chapter Four, come back to this page and see if you can complete the list above.

Using the hi-hat pedal

So far we've only focused on three-way co-ordination, using both hands and one foot. There is, however, another pedal that operates the hi-hats, which we have so far ignored. It's now time to start developing our four-way co-ordination. Using the hi-hat pedal will create a variety of new sounds and effects, add more depth and texture to our playing and make it even more musical.

The three main ways of using the hi-hat pedal are:

1. Hi-hat intensity and volume control: Control the hi-hat sound for complete sections of music
2. Hi-hat lifts: Open the hi-hats in time with, or in between specific beats
3. Stepped hi-hats: Keeping a constant stepped hi-hat (covered in the Level 2 book)

Hi-hat intensity

While playing grooves on the hi-hats, we can use the hi-hat pedal to create many different sounds, ranging from tightly closed and controlled to loose and sloppy (sometimes called 'trashy'). This technique adds different feels to entire sections of music, or can build intensity and volume within a section by gradually moving between sounds.

Open your hi-hats by about an inch and then to get used to the different sounds you can create, play a basic eighth note groove and apply different levels of pressure to the pedal. For a tight sound, push more of your weight into your toes, whereas for a trashy sound, push more weight into your heel.

The two grooves below have different hi-hat sounds. The first has a circle above each hi-hat to denote open (trashy) hi-hats. The second has a circle with a line through above each hi-hat to denote half open hi-hats, which will create a mid way 'sizzle' sound.

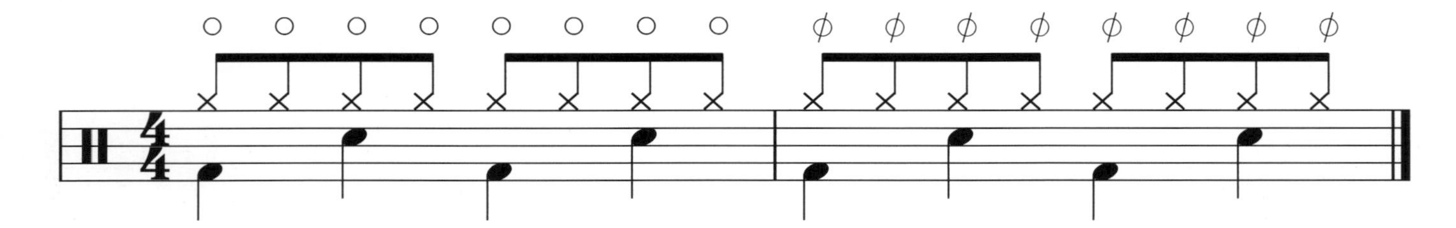

Where a groove has no markings to say open, half open or closed, you would generally play with the hi-hats closed, but use your own judgement to control the hi-hat sound to be in keeping with the music.

Technique:
As with the bass drum pedal, it is possible to operate the hi-hat pedal with either heel up (left photo) or heel down (right photo) technique.

Initially it is recommended that you play with heel down when working through the exercises in this chapter as it wiill help you to maintain balance. In the next book we look at stepped hi-hat patterns where the heel up technique works better.

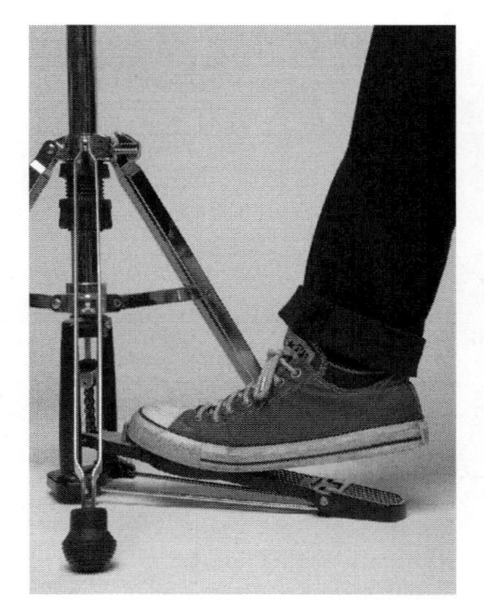

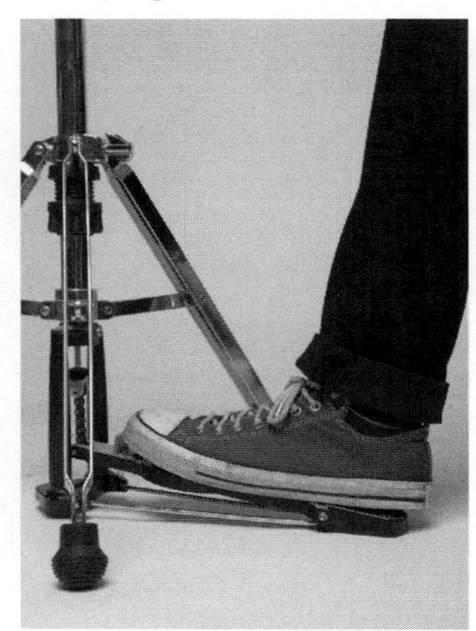

Hi-hat lifts

When playing grooves on the hi-hats, we can open and close them in time with individual beats to add extra interest and texture to grooves. This creates a 'fizz' sound. Written below are some examples of hi-hats opening and closing on and off the beat. The circle above the hi-hat line tells you when to open the hi-hat and the cross tells you when to close them again.

Off-beat hi-hat lifts

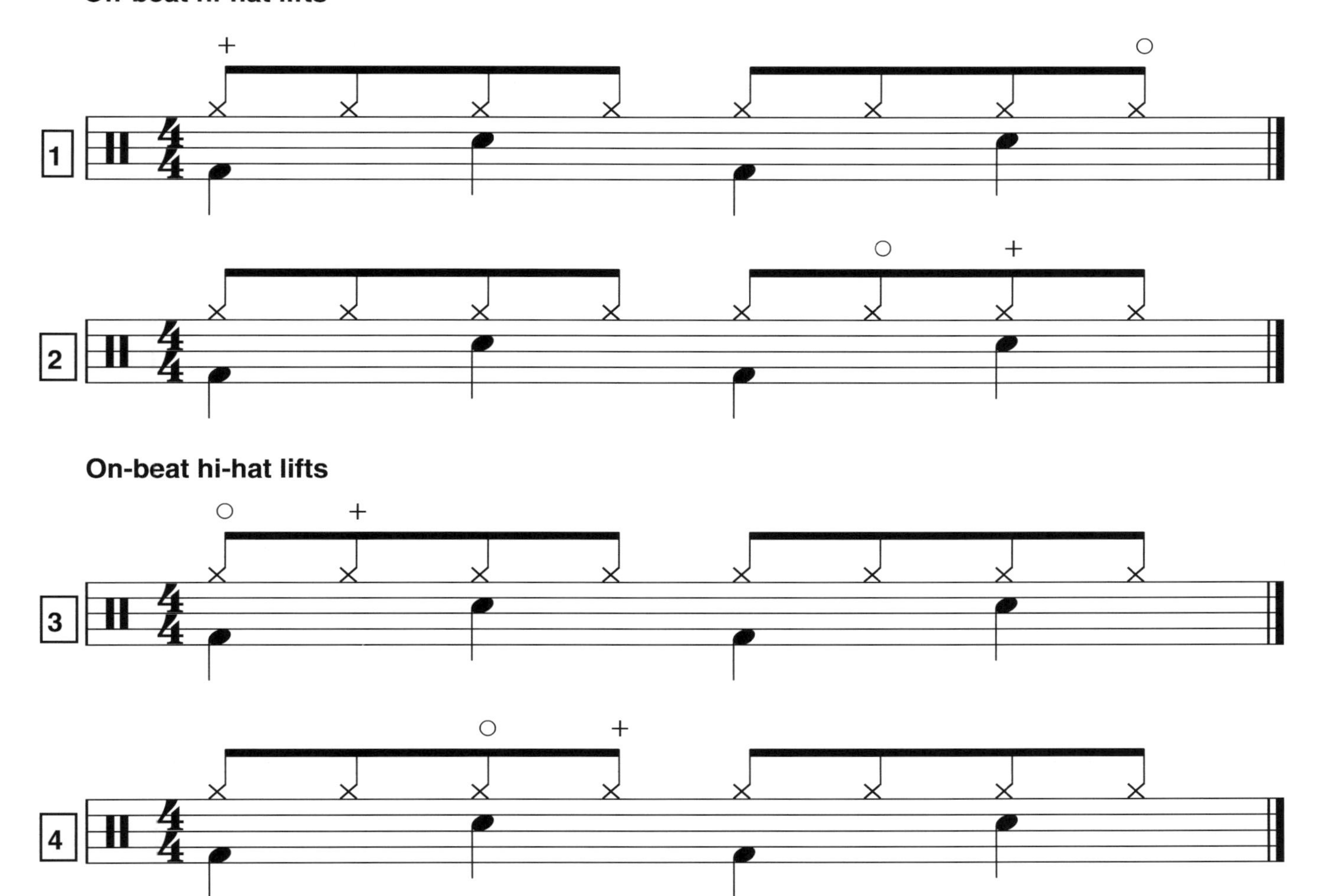

Stepped hi-hats

When playing grooves on the ride cymbal or fills around the drums, it's common to step a constant hi-hat pattern in the same way you tap your foot in time with a pulse when completing reading exercises. We won't look at this until the next book to give you time to get comfortable with the first two applications.

Signing off and moving on

Play each of the grooves above along with suitable backing tracks
Targets are in BPM

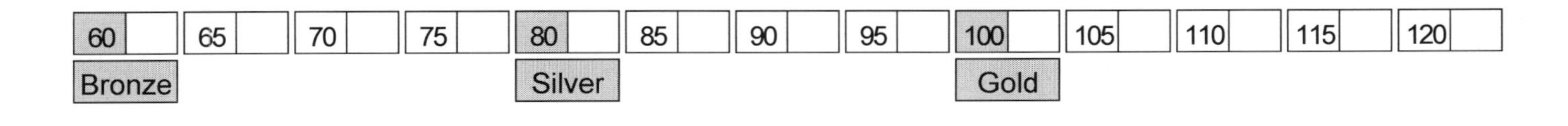

Eighth note grooves with hi-hat lifts

Now that you are starting to get used to opening and closing your hi-hats, let's have a look at some grooves with various hi-hat lifts. Play the following grooves slowly to start, then play with backing tracks and finally in four bar phrases with some simple fills.

Signing off and moving on

Play each of the grooves above along with suitable backing tracks
Targets are in BPM

60	65	70	75	80	85	90	95	100	105	110	115	120
Bronze				Silver				Gold				

Sixteenth note grooves with hi-hat lifts

With sixteenth note grooves, when opening and closing your hi-hats on or off the beat, you'll be playing two open hi-hats before you close them, as your hands are playing notes in between the on and off-beats.

Slurs: The line joining the open and closed signs are called 'slurs'. These are sometimes used to show how long a hi-hat should be left open for. The two slurs in the first bar are needed when just one bar like this is repeated.

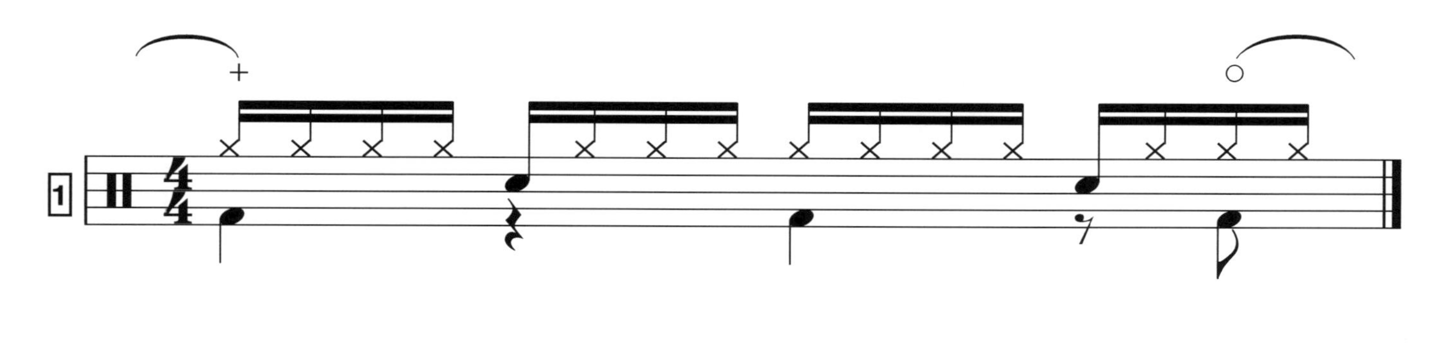

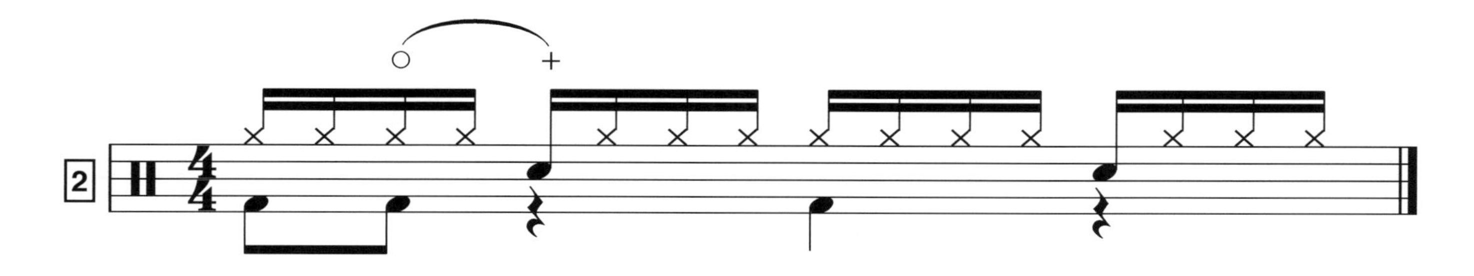

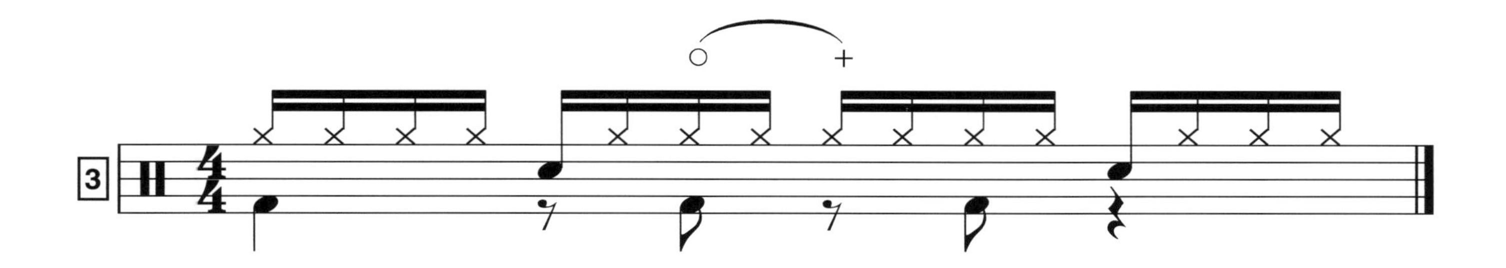

Signing off and moving on

Play each of the grooves above along with suitable backing tracks
Targets are in BPM

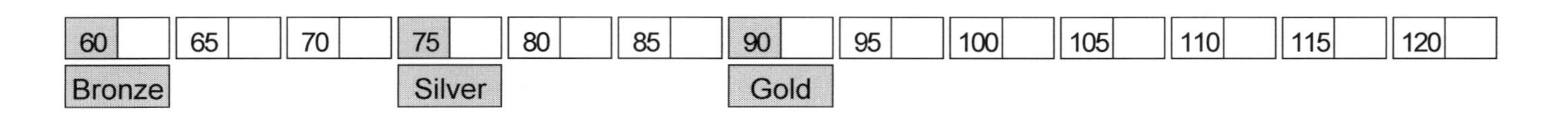

60	65	70	75	80	85	90	95	100	105	110	115	120
Bronze			Silver			Gold						

Quarter note grooves with hi-hat lifts

Opening hi-hats on the beat within quarter note grooves work really well and although maintaining an open hi-hat over two bass drums can be technically challenging, it can be very effective. The slur above the open and closed signs show how long the hi-hat has to stay open for.

Signing off and moving on

Play each of the grooves above along with suitable backing tracks
Targets are in BPM

60	65	70	75	80	85	90	95	100	105	110	115	120
Bronze						Silver						Gold

CHAPTER FIVE

All tied up

In Chapter Five, we look at what happens when you 'tie' notes together.

Half note (minim) and quarter note (crotchet) tied

Checklist

By the end of this chapter, you should be able to achieve the following:

- Work out the effect of different note values being tied together
- Understand and correctly play exercises containing tied notes

Use this page as an end-of-chapter test. When you've completed Chapter Five, come back to this page and see if you can complete the list above.

Tied notes

A tie looks very similar to a slur but has a totally different meaning.

Tying notes together adds their values to create one longer note. This is more commonly used in music written for instruments with sustain, such as a trumpet, as they may need to hold a note that lasts an odd length for which there is no single note value available.

The effect of a note with ties is very easy to work out. If two or more notes are tied together you play just the first note, but add the value of the other notes to it. Here are a few examples to help explain this:

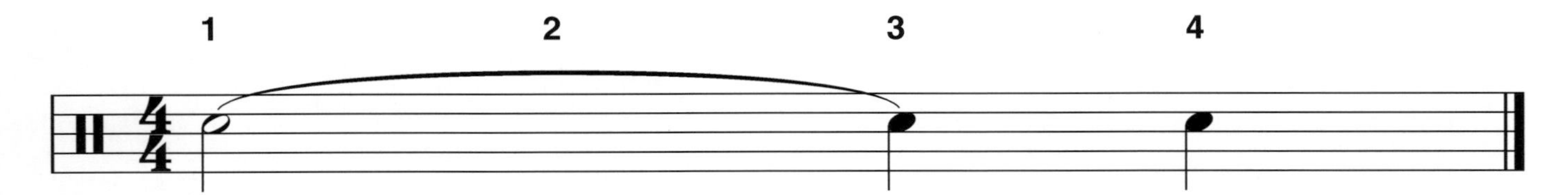

The half note on count 1 lasts for two counts, and the quarter note on count 3 lasts for one count. These notes are tied together so their values are added, making a note that lasts three counts. (The value of the second note has been added to that of the first).

The quarter notes on counts 1 and 2 last one count each, but as they are tied together only the first note is played, making one note that lasts for two counts. (The value of the second note has been added to that of the first).

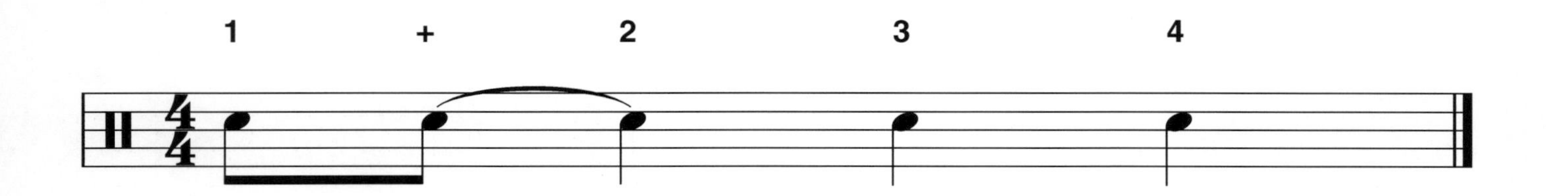

The eighth note in between counts 1 and 2 only lasts for half a count, but as it's tied to the quarter note on count 2 that lasts for one count, their values are added making a note that lasts for one and a half counts. (The value of the note on count 2 has been added to that of the '+' of 1).

Tied notes for drums

When playing drums, the length of the note generally does not make a difference to the sound we create as we cannot control the length of the note. When reading music that has tied notes, we have to imagine that note lasting and wait for the correct amount of time before playing the next note. This also means that we will see things written in different ways which would sound different on other instruments, but will actually sound the same on drums.

The four bars below look totally different and if played on an instrument with sustain, would sound totally different. When played on a drum, they all sound the same.

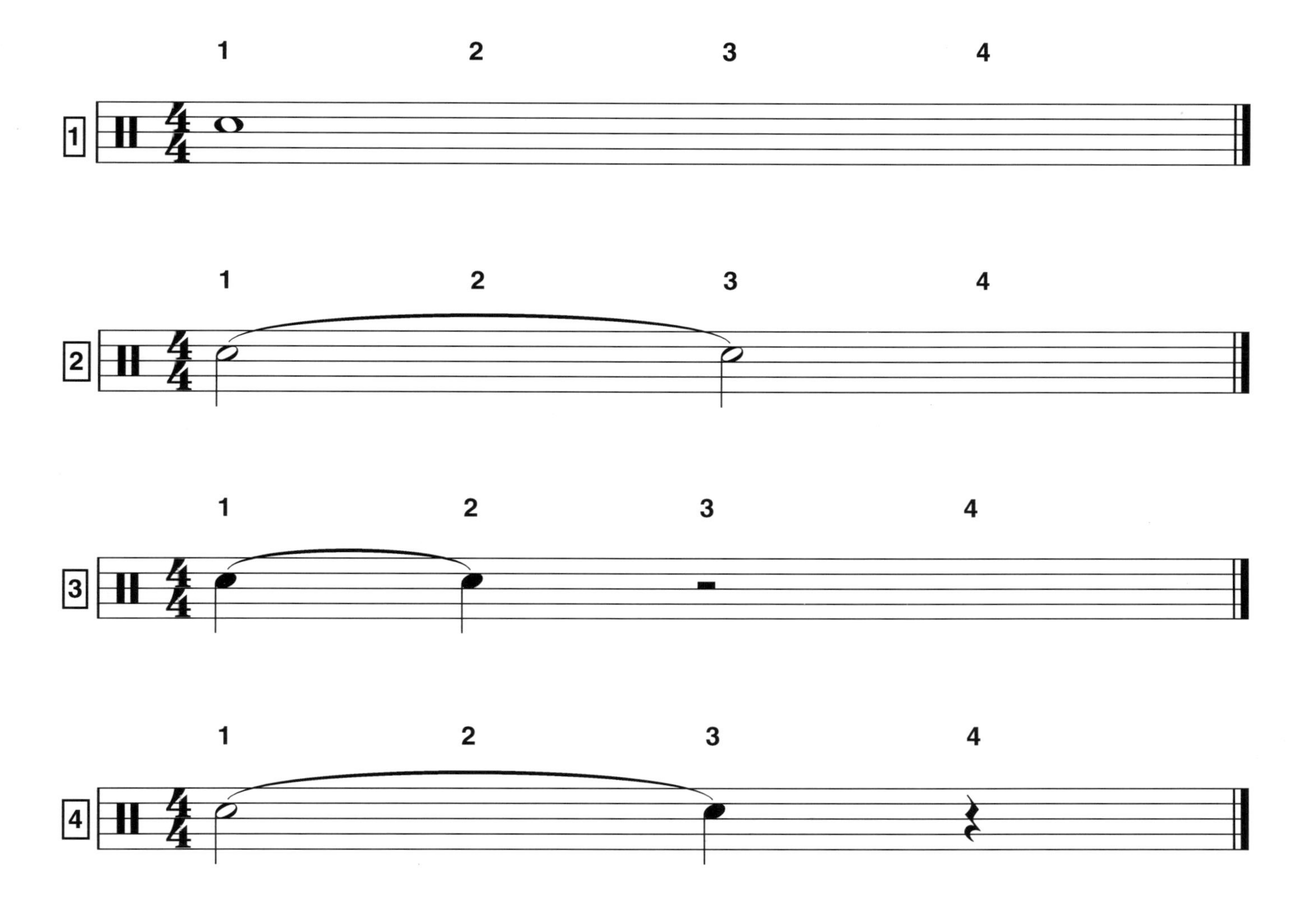

Tied note examples

Now that you understand how ties work, you may think that as drummers this isn't very relevant to our playing, however, you will see ties in drum music for certain situations. The most common use of ties in drum music is when a cymbal is required to ring on, or if a push at the end of a bar is to continue into the next bar.

Look at the following examples.

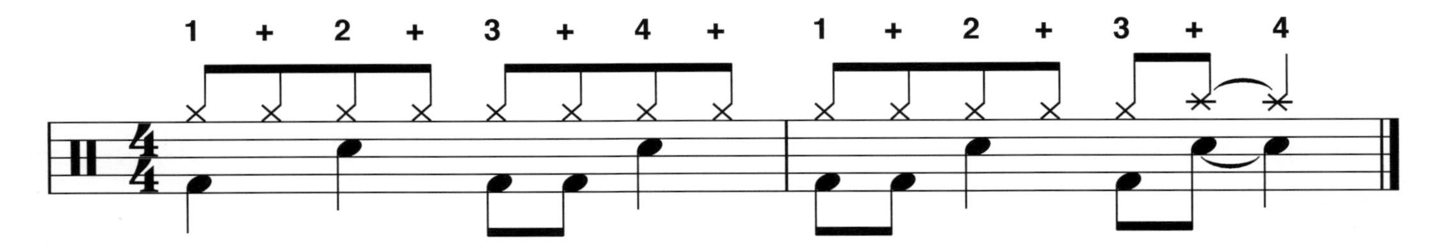

This example could be the last bar of a song and ends on the 'and' of three. If there was a rest on the cymbal line on count four, you may assume that it's to be quiet and therefore choke the cymbal immediately after hitting it. By tying it to another quarter note, you know not to play on count 4, but you also know that the cymbal is required to ring on for the remainder of the bar.

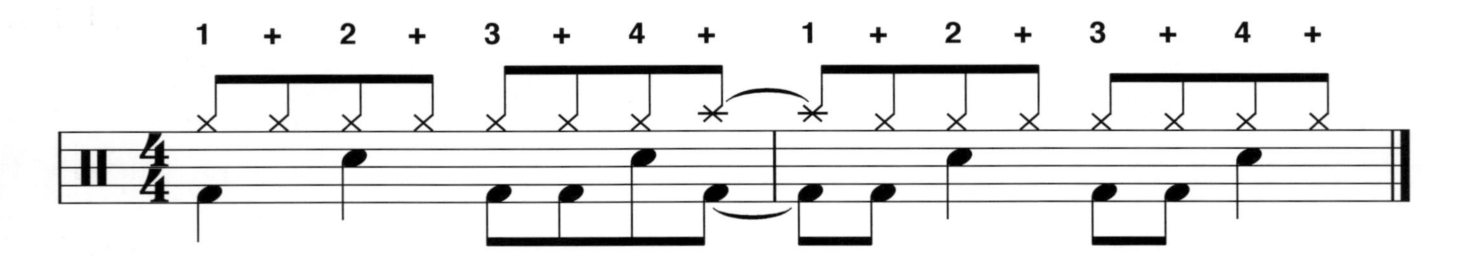

This example could be from a section of a song with some big pushes at the end of every other bar. Here you are required to play a crash and a bass drum at the end of the first bar, which hangs over to the next bar. If these notes were not tied, you would play the first notes in the second bar, which wouldn't give the crash enough space to be very powerful. If there was a rest on beat one in the second bar, you would assume that it's supposed to be quiet and catch the cymbal straight after hitting it again not giving the crash enough space to be very powerful.

Signing off and moving on

Play each of the two bar phrases above along with a click track or suitable backing tracks
Targets are in BPM

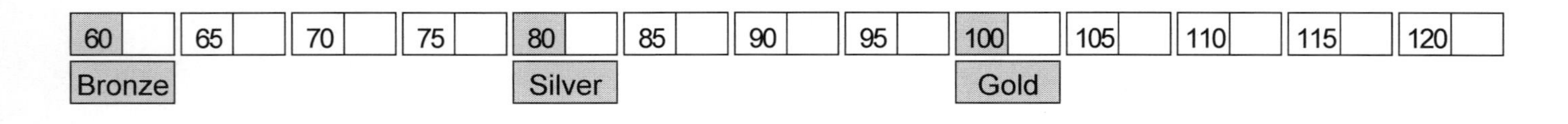

60	65	70	75	80	85	90	95	100	105	110	115	120
Bronze				Silver				Gold				

You gotta have style

Blues and disco

Moving on from the last book, we now look at two more different styles of music.

Checklist

By the end of this chapter, you should be able to achieve the following:

- Understand and identify the main characteristics of blues music
- Understand and identify the main characteristics of disco music
- Understand the concept of feel in music and apply it to your playing

Use this page as an end-of-chapter test. When you've completed Chapter Six, come back to this page and see if you can complete the list above.

Blues Music

History:
Blues music originated from within the African American communities of the deep South USA in the late 1800's and has its roots in the spiritual and work songs of the period. Through a struggle for the end of slavery and the beginning of a new freedom for black Americans, times were tough and often quite depressing and the music reflected this. People said that if you were depressed, you were suffering from the 'blue devils' so that is how 'blues' gets its name. As a style of music it has endured right through to the present day and has influenced many other modern styles of music including rock n' roll, jazz, pop, R&B, gospel, funk and hip hop.

Sound:
Traditional blues music typically has a sad or depressing feel to it and can quite often be quite slow and lazy. Songs follow a very specific format based around a 'walking' bass guitar line, mostly based around triplets, that resolves over a certain number of bars. The most common format is the twelve bar blues which contains the three basics chords (I, IV and V), but there are also similar eight and sixteen bar versions. Lyrics often describe a depressed mood and cover subjects such as lost love, cruelty of the police, economic depression and hard times. The singing technique used is more of a rhythmic talk than a traditional song, and is possibly a forerunner of modern rap music.

About:
The earliest blues music came from slave work songs and field hollers which were a type of call and response. Similar to a question and answer, one person shouts a line and another individual or group responds with another line. When mixed with European musical influences this call and response changed to be between vocals and instruments such as a guitar or harmonica. As blues developed more instruments were used, the most common of which include drums, piano, trumpet and bass guitar.

Sub genres:
For a genre of music that has been around for so long there are far too many sub genres to list but here are a few:

Blues rock – Blues jazz – Country blues – Urban blues – Delta blues – Piedmont blues – Jump blues – Chicago blues – Electric blues – Boogie woogie – Soul blues – Gospel blues – Louisiana blues

Recommended listening:
With a genre of music such as blues, there are so many artists covering so many periods and sub genres that it's impossible to write a short list that covers it all. Here are just a few to get you started:

Bessie Smith – Howlin' Wolf – Charlie Patton – Blind Willie Johnson – Mamie Smith – Dr John – T-Bone Walker – Muddy Waters – John Lee Hooker – BB King – Robert Johnson – Eric Clapton – Bonnie Raitt

Signing off and moving on

List two characteristics of blues music, four instruments commonly used and two famous blues artists

Disco Music

History:
Disco music is a form of dance music popular in the 1970's that was strongly influenced by music such as funk, soul and latin music. Disco music originated in the late 1960's but the term 'disco' was first used in 1973 and was derived from the French word 'discotheque' meaning library of records. It remained in the mainstream right through the 1970's until a massive anti-disco campaign by rock fans in the early 1980's saw to its demise. Despite being in the mainstream for only a few years it has been highly influential on such genres as pop, electro, techno, house, hip hop and rave. Originally created by real musicians with traditional instruments, towards the end of the 1970's things got more experimental and was one of the first genres of music to use electronic drums and synthesizers and paved the way for the 1980's electro movement.

Sound:
Disco music was designed to make people dance and because of that a lot of the elements that make up disco songs are very simple and repetitive. There was also an emphasis on recordings of disco songs which were played in discotheques meaning that lots of layers of music with a real variety of instruments could be used. Common instruments heard include drums, electric rhythm guitar, electric bass guitar, keyboards, synthesizers, horns (trumpets, saxophone, trombone etc), strings (harp, violin, cello etc), latin percussion, flute etc. Drums help to give disco its feel by playing simple rhythms which could include four to the floor bass drum patterns, off-beat hi-hats and sixteenth note grooves. Lyrics in disco songs vary greatly from topics such as love and romance to politics and social situations.

About:
The disco era and the time of the discotheque also gave birth to many things taken for granted today such as night clubs with impressive sound and lighting systems, and DJs mixing records and becoming musicians in their own right. The rave culture of the 1990's and today's clubbing scene is also said to be the modern day equivalent of the disco scene. In the 2000's there was a disco revival, with the re-release of classic disco albums and today many artists from all sorts of genres incorporate elements of disco into their music.

Sub genres:
Proto disco – Electronic disco – Symphonic disco – Italo disco – Electro – Electro funk – Garage – Hi-NRG – Disco rap – Disco rock – Synthpop – Freestyle – Post disco – Nu disco

Recommended listening:
ABBA – Jackson five – Bee Gees – Boney M – Donna Summer (the Queen of disco) – Diana Ross – Sister Sledge – early Michael Jackson – KC and the Sunshine band – Gloria Gaynor

Signing off and moving on

List two characteristics of disco music, four instruments commonly used and two famous disco artists

Feel in music

Feel in music is created by the way we play our instruments in a musical way. We have a lot of control over how our grooves and fills sound by either employing different techniques to create different sounds, by playing harder or softer to achieve different volumes, by adjusting our hi-hat sounds or by playing ever so slightly ahead or behind the beat to create a rushed or a lazy feel.

How we play:
We spend so much of our time practicing what to play, we quite often forget to think about how we play and this is a mistake. In a band situation, a drummer's job is to keep time for that band and to add musically to the songs being played. It is far better to play simple ideas with perfect timing and great feel, rather than playing overly complicated parts with less than perfect timing and no feel. A band is a team and everyone has their part to play to make the music the best it can be. As drummers we have a huge effect on how the music sounds by having perfect timing, but as musicians we have a huge effect on the over all sound of the music by getting the right feel.

Applying feel in music to drums:
When playing music you need to think about how that music makes you feel so that you can put that feeling into your playing. This is a very complex subject and one that will make more sense the more you play, but for now there are just a few pointers to get you thinking like a musician.

- Listening to a slow blues song with a very sad feel to it, may conjure up images in your head of a sad event or make you feel very lazy and lethargic. If you take this into your playing and play with a lazy feel using simple grooves and fills you will be close to capturing the feel of the song and help to make it feel good. As a contrast, if you ignore the feel of the music and aim to play the most complicated beats and fills you can with lots of energy and power, your playing will not fit in with the music at all and you are in danger of killing the music for everyone by applying the wrong feel.

- The opposite example would be when listening to a fast aggressive rock tune, you might conjure up images similar to that of a fast paced action movie with lots of energy. To keep that in mind and play drums with full energy and power would fit in, whereas the feel you would have applied to the blues tune above would be completely wrong and would make the song drag and again feel wrong.

Music videos:
Music videos are a great way for bands and artists to help promote and sell their music, again the wrong video choice for a song could have a bad effect as that also adds to the feel of the music. If you had a beautiful, slow love song and you put a video of a car chase through a city, it wouldn't work. Just as an up-beat dance tune with a video of an old man on a rocking chair wouldn't work either. A good way to develop your understanding of this concept and to appreciate the feel of music more, is to listen to a mixture of songs and imagine what the music video would be like for each. Try playing along with some of these songs while thinking of the music video you have imagined and see how it can effect the way you play.

Signing off and moving on

Play along to two different songs of your choice and demonstrate a different feel for each

Charting success

That's the end of the main lessons, so in Chapter Seven, there are some charts for you to read and play along with. The music here contains elements that you've covered in this book and the Foundation Book.

Checklist

By the end of this chapter, you should be able to achieve the following:

- Understand and play grooves and fills using eighth note triplets
- Understand and play grooves and fills using sixteenth notes
- Play rudiments over eighth notes, eighth note triplets and sixteenth notes
- Understand and play grooves and fills using off-beat eighth notes
- Use your hi-hat pedal to add interest and musicality to your playing
- Understand and play tied notes
- Apply feel to your playing

If you are happy with everything so far, you can now work through the charts in this chapter and then move on to Backbone Drums Level Two.

Grade exams

If you are interested in taking exams in music, you have now covered enough material to take a grade one exam. Talk to your teacher about what you need to do after completing this final chapter.

Chart One: reading eighth note triplets

Signing off and moving on

Play the entire page as one exercise along with a click track
Targets are in BPM

60	65	70	75	80	85	90	95	100	105	110	115	120
Bronze						Silver						Gold

Chart Two: triplet blues (65bpm)

Track 18: With drums
Track 19: With click

Count in: 1 - 2 - 1-2-3-4

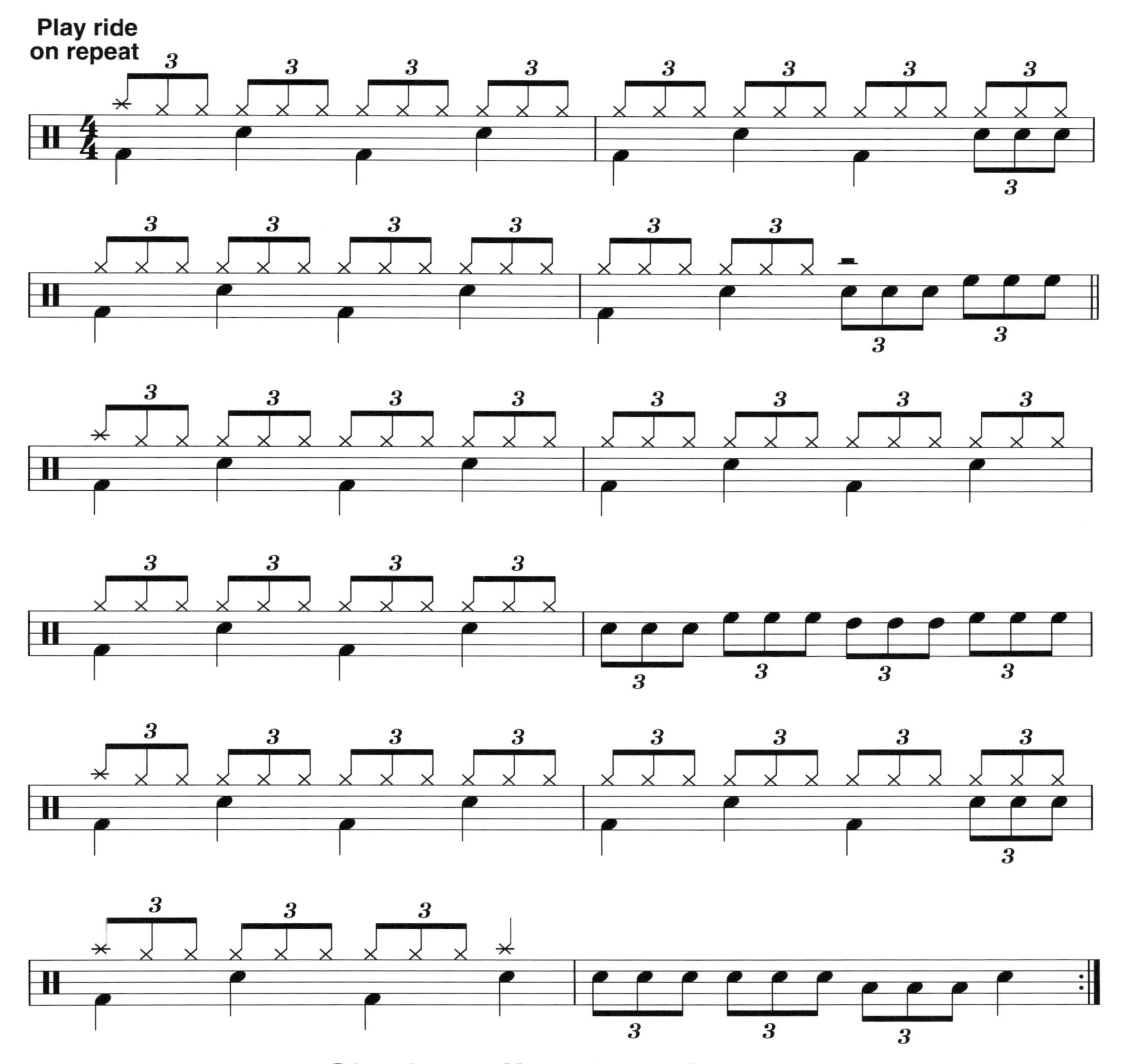

Signing off and moving on

Play the chart with backing track Number 19

Gold: Good timing and no mistakes
Silver: Good timing and with three or fewer mistakes
Bronze: Acceptable timing with three or fewer mistakes

Chart Three: reading sixteenth notes

Signing off and moving on

Play the entire page as one exercise along with a click track
Targets are in BPM

60	65	70	75	80	85	90	95	100	105	110	115	120
Bronze						Silver						Gold

Chart Four: sixteenth note rock (75bpm)

Track 20: With drums
Track 21: With click

Count in: 1 - 2 - 1-2-3-4

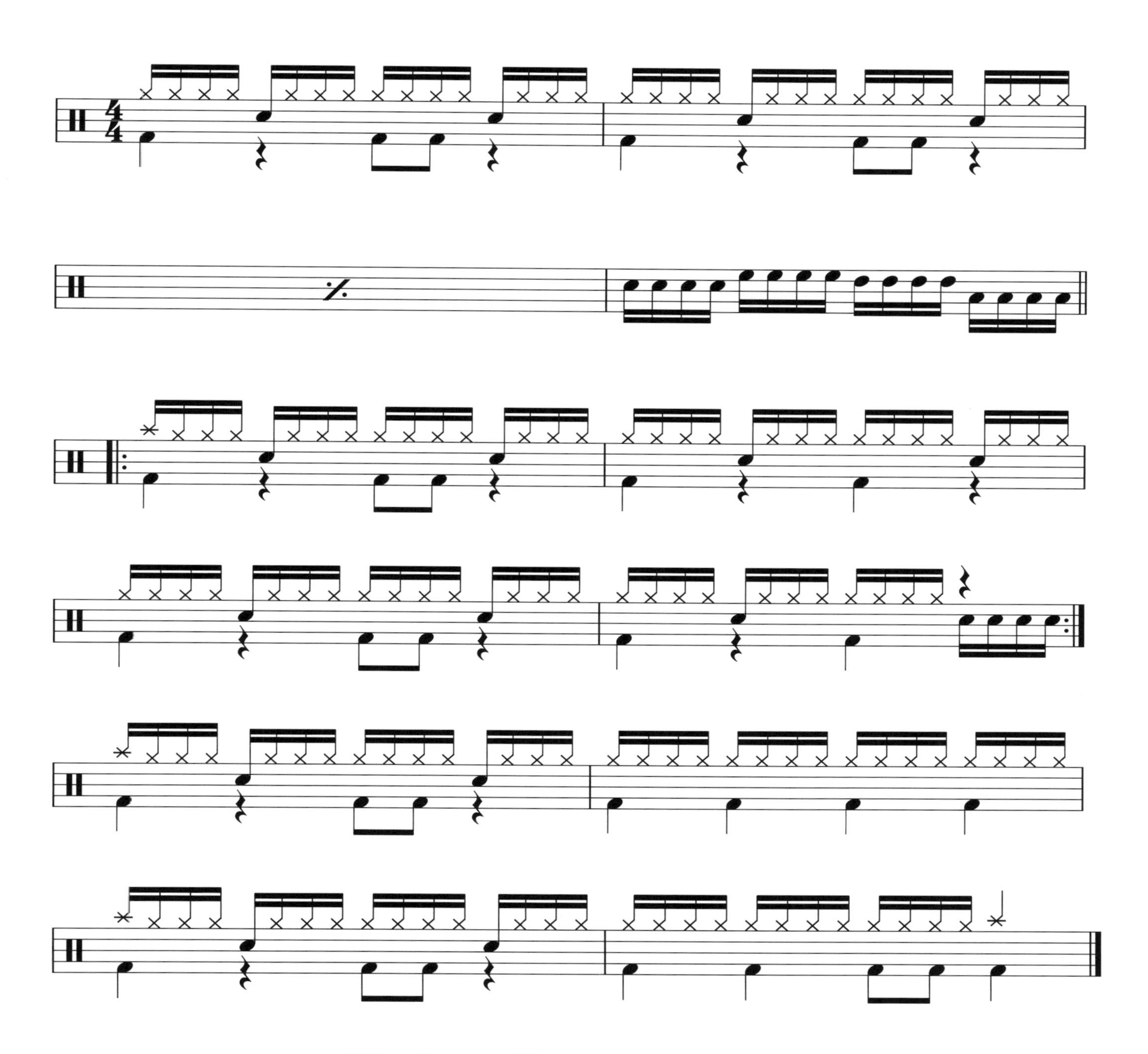

Signing off and moving on

Play the chart with backing track Number 21

Gold: Good timing and no mistakes
Silver: Good timing and with three or fewer mistakes
Bronze: Acceptable timing with three or fewer mistakes

Chart Five: reading off-beat rhythms

Signing off and moving on

Play the entire page as one exercise along with a click track

Targets are in BPM

60	65	70	75	80	85	90	95	100	105	110	115	120
Bronze						Silver						Gold

Chart Six: off-beat disco (100bpm)

Track 22: With drums
Track 23: With click

Count in: 1 - 2 - 1-2-3-4

Signing off and moving on

Play the chart with backing track Number 23

Gold: Good timing and no mistakes
Silver: Good timing and with three or fewer mistakes
Bronze: Acceptable timing with three or fewer mistakes

Chart Seven: mixed rhythm rock (110bpm)

Track 24: With drums
Track 25: With click

Count in: 1 - 2 - 1-2-3-4

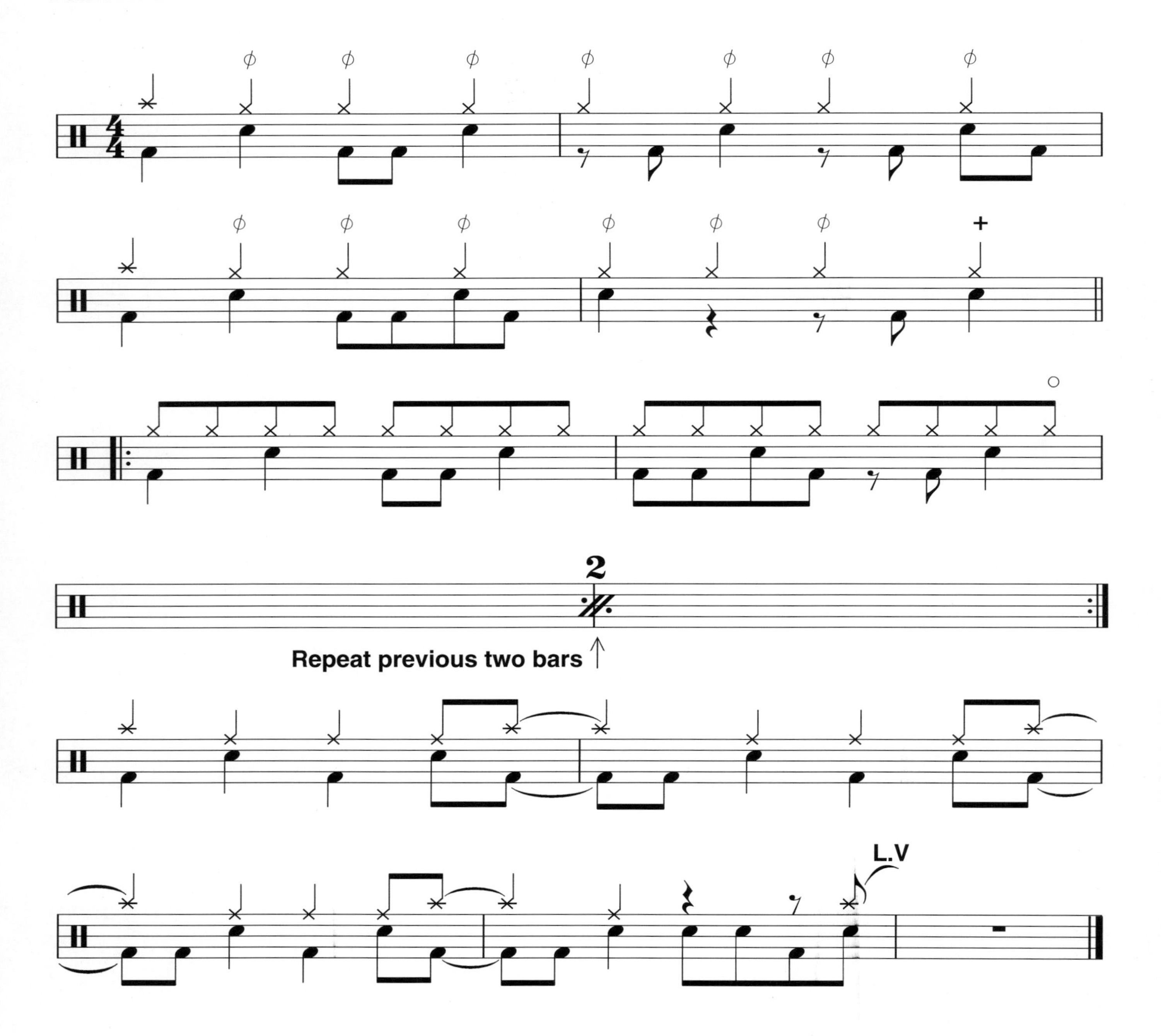

Signing off and moving on

Play the chart with backing track Number 25

Gold: Good timing and no mistakes
Silver: Good timing and with three or fewer mistakes
Bronze: Acceptable timing with three or fewer mistakes